Lent with Luke

David Thomson

Lent with Luke

David Thomson

Authentic
LIFESTYLE

First published 2005 by Authentic Lifestyle

Authentic Lifestyle is an imprint of Authentic Media,
P.O. Box 300, Carlisle, Cumbria, CA3 0QS, U.K.
and
P.O. Box 1047, Waynesboro, GA 30830-2047, U.S.A.

11 10 09 08 07 06 05   7 6 5 4 3 2 1

British Library Cataloguing in Publication Data
A catalogue record for this book is available from the British Library

ISBN 1-85078-597-X

Designed and typeset by Christopher Lawther, Teamwork, Lancing, West Sussex
and printed and bound in Great Britain by Bell and Bain, Glasgow

Contents

Preface   viii

Week 1   **THE STORY BEGINS**
Shrove Tuesday   1.1-4   This is our Story   1
Ash Wednesday   1.5-25   A Birth is Announced   2
Thursday   1.26-38   The Annunciation   4
Friday   1.39-45   The Visitation   6
Saturday   2.1-21   Nativity   8
Study material   10

Week 2   **THE CALL OF CHRIST**
First Sunday of Lent   11
Monday   5.1-11   The Call of the Disciples   12
Tuesday   5.27-32   The Call of Levi   14
Wednesday   6.12-16   The Twelve   16
Thursday   9.1-9   Sent out   18
Friday   9.18-27   At Caesarea Philippi   20
Saturday   9.28-45   The Transfiguration   22
Study material   24

Week 3   **STORIES ON THE WAY**
Second Sunday of Lent   25
Monday   10.25-37   The Good Samaritan   26
Tuesday   12.13-21   The Rich Fool   28
Wednesday   14.15-24   The Great Banquet   30
Thursday   15.11-32   The Lost Son   32
Friday   16.1-15   The Shrewd Manager   34
Saturday   16.19-31   The Rich Man and Lazarus   36
Study material   38

Week 4   JERUSALEM, JERUSALEM

Third Sunday of Lent			39
Monday	18.31-34	To Jerusalem	40
Tuesday	19.1-10	Zacchaeus	42
Wednesday	19.28-44	Triumphal Entry	44
Thursday	19.45-48	Cleansing the Temple	46
Friday	21.1-14	The Widow's Mite	48
Saturday	21.5-11	Signs of the End	50
Study material			52

Week 5   THE HOUR HAS COME

Fourth Sunday of Lent *Mothering Sunday*			53
Monday	22.1-6	The Tempter Returns	54
Tuesday	22.7-23	Then Came the Day	56
Wednesday	22.24-34	Table Talk	58
Thursday	22.35-46	Gethsemane	60
Friday	22.47-53	The Heart of Darkness	62
Saturday	22.54-62	The Look of Christ's Love	64
Study material			66

Week 6   BEHOLD THE MAN

Fifth Sunday of Lent *Passion Sunday*			67
Monday	22.63-71	The Man of Sorrows	68
Tuesday	22.63-64	Dignity and Disability	70
Wednesday	23.1-5	Man of Righteousness	72
Thursday	23.6-12	Before Herod	74
Friday	23.13-22	The Weakness of Pilate	76
Saturday	23.23-25	Handed Over	78
Study material			80

Week 7 *Holy Week*   THE VICTORY OF THE CROSS
Sixth Sunday of Lent *Palm Sunday*   81
Monday   23.26-31   A Very Public Passion   82
Tuesday   contd.   Before the Cross   84
Wednesday   23.32-43   A Pointed Question   86
Maundy Thursday   23.44-47   What is our Witness?   88
Good Friday   23.48-56   Not the End - the Beginning   90
Easter Eve   23.54-56   Preparation Day   92
Study material   94

Easter Week   TO ALL NATIONS
Easter Day   24.1-8   Alleluia!   95
Easter Monday   24.9-12   Only Believe   96
Easter Tuesday   24.13-35   The Lord has Risen   98
Easter Wednesday   24.36-43   The Peace of His Presence   100
Easter Thursday   24.44-48   The Scriptures Fulfilled   102
Easter Friday   24.49-53   Waiting for the Spirit   104

References   106
Further Reading   110
List of illustrations   112

Contents   **vii**

Preface

Lent is a time for growing in our faith. The word Lent itself comes from a root meaning the 'lengthening' days of spring. The gloomy atmosphere with which we invest it is not entirely appropriate – even if growth often requires some pruning first. So this is an opportunity to reach down more deeply into the Good News, and reach up more fully into the new life it brings.

In this book you are invited to 'lengthen' your faith by sharing Lent with St Luke, reading a part of his Gospel each day. At its heart is the Passion Narrative which we follow as Easter approaches. Before that we look at a selection of passages from the earlier part of Luke's Gospel, chosen to let its whole story speak into the story of our lives. The daily studies start on Shrove Tuesday, and – perhaps unusually for a Lent book – run through into the week after Easter. The point here is that our own story of faith does not suddenly stop on Easter Day, but like Luke's story carries on into the Acts of our life through the year.

Luke, so legend has it, was an artist as well as doctor.* There are I think seven paintings of the Blessed Virgin Mary that are claimed as his! De Vos' (reproduced opposite) is one of the best known. The unlikely presence of an ox in the equally unlikely grand room suggests we are not dealing with literal reality here ... Whatever the truth of the legend, this book has deliberately used paintings of the gospel scenes not because they give accurate depictions but because they help us look with fresh eyes and make us think again. What do you think de Vos, for instance, is trying to say?

I grew up in urban Sheffield in the days before the Clean Air Act, and vividly remember feeling my way to school through the yellow smog. Perhaps it was because of the drabness of the surroundings then that colour, nature and art broke into my world so forcefully just a few years ago. Moving to the grandeur and wide open spaces of Cumbria must have had something to do with it as well. Modern Scottish art with its high-key palette was the appetizer, then the great galleries, and finally an adventurous chase through the history of the Gospel in art.

de Vos,
St Luke
painting
the Virgin

While all this was going on, my 'day job' of an abiding quest to bring together the Gospel and daily life in preaching and prayer, learning and living was continuing. Inevitably the two themes met, especially as I dug for material to use on the quiet days and retreats that I am often asked to lead. And so this book was born.

I have used the language of 'story' extensively through the studies in describing both the gospel and our own lives – taking the hint again from Luke, the historian, of course, but also reading the Bible myself as someone who grew up with literature, went on to study it, and is still fascinated by the interplay between our creativity and that of God, the Author of all.

Each weekday study, then, offers a Bible passage to read; a comment – often with a reproduction of a painting or part of a painting to accompany it; and then a prayer, sometimes a classic, sometimes one of my own.

Shrove Tuesday and the Sundays in Lent have shorter studies, more a thought to 'Start the Week' which also has some relationship to the Collect and lectionary readings for the day which some readers will be using. This is all on the assumption that you will be well fed in church on Sunday and concentrating on what is on offer there!

At the end of each week you will find a few suggestions for study, either on your own or in a group. I have kept these quite short, so you may need extra material if you are basing a whole evening round them – but we more often err by fitting in too much rather than doing too little on such occasions.

I have used the metaphor of a meal for the study suggestions – a starter, main course and dessert – to give a simple but hopefully tasty outline to follow. The book designer has added some attractive icons to steer you through! You may want to start each time by lighting a candle, opening your Bible, and praying for the help of the Spirit – and each dessert will lead you back into prayer as well.

I have given full references and copyright details for the illustrations in a separate section at the end of the book – space was too tight to put these beside the illustrations themselves. As reasons of cost have sadly meant that the illustrations are in greyscale, I have also given web links which will lead you to colour versions which you can use in your study, subject of course to any copyright restrictions.

Thanks to Jeremy Mudditt for his production work and encouragment, Chris Lawther for the design, and the people at Authentic for their forbearance in an unusual project; to Molly and Graham Dow, my father Ron, and many others who have helped with comment and criticism; to the clergy and people of Cumbria who unwittingly road-tested some of the material when it was even rougher than it is now; and above all to Jean and our family who let me get on with it but never get away with it.

David Thomson

USING THIS BOOK

 Bible passage

 Starter

 Meditation

 Main Course

 Prayer

 Dessert

* **References** (see pages 106-109)

SHROVE TUESDAY
THE STORY BEGINS

This is our Story

Luke 1.1-4

Many have undertaken to draw up an account of the things that have been fulfilled among us, just as they were handed down to us by those who from the first were eyewitnesses and servants of the word. Therefore, since I myself have carefully investigated everything from the beginning, it seemed good also to me to write an orderly account for you, most excellent Theophilus, so that you may know the certainty of the things you have been taught.

Luke is often seen as the historian among the gospel makers. There is a richness of sources and a carefulness of detail that fit well with the claim in the prologue. But Luke's concern, to use an old pun, is not so much with history in its modern academic sense as with his story, the (indeed historical) story of God's unfolding plan for the world.

The phrase 'servants of the word' in Luke's introduction is also the word for the village storytellers of the Middle East. I remember seeing such a storyteller from Iraq presenting the tale of Alexander the Great with immense vigour,* as if it was as contemporary as the recent war in Iraq. History, but more than history – a living story of the people's identity still.

In the same way we open up again the great story of Jesus the Christ, well-known already, and well-founded in history, not just to know it, but to be inspired by it in the faith that changes us and changes the world to this day. As you get ready to keep Lent with Luke take a moment to recollect the vastness of the story of the creation and redemption of our amazing universe. History, his story, and our story too.

This is our story
This is our song
Hosanna in the highest

COMMON WORSHIP, Eucharistic Prayer D *

ASH WEDNESDAY
A Birth is Announced

Luke 1:5-25

In the time of Herod king of Judea there was a priest named Zechariah, who belonged to the priestly division of Abijah; his wife Elizabeth was also a descendant of Aaron. Both of them were upright in the sight of God, observing all the Lord's commandments and regulations blamelessly. But they had no children, because Elizabeth was barren; and they were both well along in years.

Once when Zechariah's division was on duty and he was serving as priest before God, he was chosen by lot, according to the custom of the priesthood, to go into the temple of the Lord and burn incense. And when the time for the burning of incense came, all the assembled worshipers were praying outside.

Then an angel of the Lord appeared to him, standing at the right side of the altar of incense. When Zechariah saw him, he was startled and was gripped with fear. But the angel said to him: 'Do not be afraid, Zechariah; your prayer has been heard. Your wife Elizabeth will bear you a son, and you are to give him the name John. He will be a joy and delight to you, and many will rejoice because of his birth, for he will be great in the sight of the Lord. He is never to take wine or other fermented drink, and he will be filled with the Holy Spirit even from birth. Many of the people of Israel will he bring back to the Lord their God. And he will go on before the Lord, in the spirit and power of Elijah, to turn the hearts of the fathers to their children and the disobedient to the wisdom of the righteous – to make ready a people prepared for the Lord.'

Zechariah asked the angel, 'How can I be sure of this? I am an old man and my wife is well along in years.'

The angel answered, 'I am Gabriel. I stand in the presence of God, and I have been sent to speak to you and to tell you this good news. And now you will be silent and not able to speak until the day this happens, because you did not believe my words, which will come true at their proper time.'

Meanwhile, the people were waiting for Zechariah and wondering why he stayed so long in the temple. When he came out, he could not speak to them. They realized he had seen a vision in the temple, for he kept making signs to them but remained unable to speak.

When his time of service was completed, he returned home. After this his wife Elizabeth became pregnant and for five months remained in seclusion. 'The Lord has done this for me,' she said. 'In these days he has shown his favour and taken away my disgrace among the people.'

Luke's gospel begins and ends in the Temple – but what a tale lies between. Zechariah and Elizabeth are the salt of the earth, 'The Quiet in the Land' as they were sometimes known: faithful people waiting for the Messiah without thought of provoking his coming through violence. But their religion is conventional and their level of immediate expectation low. Suddenly Zechariah has the once in a lifetime chance to burn incense in the temple itself. In that special moment God speaks to him through an angel. The Holy Spirit is on the move. Will Zechariah bend to His will and take his part in the story?

To help him do that Zechariah needs a time of silence and waiting. This can be a model for us during Lent – more listening, less rehearsing our own thoughts; more looking to see what God is doing. Zechariah's waiting led to a birth: ours can lead to fruitfulness too.

Our studies these first few days are all about getting ready for the journey which lies ahead. Are you ready to 'let go and let God', to trust him, and expect good things from him? It's not always easy. Could you try writing your own Lenten prayer that captures your own feelings about this?

How many times, Lord, have I stood in your temple
And just let the worship pass me by?
So many aches in my body, So many things on my mind,
So much to organise, So much to get done.
And then suddenly,
A presence, an angel, A thickening of the air
And a deepening of the Spirit.
Thank you Lord,
That when I am far off
You are always there
To find me.

WEEK 1: *The Story Begins*   **3**

The Annunciation

Fra Lippo Lippi, *The Annunciation*

Luke 1.26-38

In the sixth month, God sent the angel Gabriel to Nazareth, a town in Galilee, to a virgin pledged to be married to a man named Joseph, a descendant of David. The virgin's name was Mary. The angel went to her and said, 'Greetings, you who are highly favoured! The Lord is with you.'

Mary was greatly troubled at his words and wondered what kind of greeting this might be. But the angel said to her, 'Do not be afraid, Mary, you have found favour with God. You will be with child and give birth to a son, and you are to give him the name Jesus. He will be great and will be called the Son of the Most High. The Lord God will give him the throne of his father David, and he will reign over the house of Jacob forever; his kingdom will never end.'

'How will this be,' Mary asked the angel, 'since I am a virgin?'

The angel answered, 'The Holy Spirit will come upon you, and the power of the Most High will overshadow you. So the holy one to be born will be called the Son of God. Even Elizabeth your relative is going to have a child in her old age, and she who was said to be barren is in her sixth month. For nothing is impossible with God.'

'I am the Lord's servant,' Mary answered. 'May it be to me as you have said.' Then the angel left her.

There are lots of paintings of the Annunciation. I collected them once and found that each one showed a different moment in Mary's reactions: fear, questioning, obeying, pondering ... The one by Fra Lippo Lippi reproduced here is my favourite. In its poise and balance and harmonious colour it captures the serenity of Mary's final acceptance: 'May it be to me as you have said.'

We should rightly look for peace from God when making big decisions, if we stay within his will, and I want to encourage you to trust in that. But we must also deal honestly with our fears, our questions and our doubts. Even in an encounter as direct as Mary's, discernment and acceptance are not straightforward, and we will often feel quite unsure and exposed.

The same Spirit which overshadowed Mary can also overshadow us, though, if we will accept that as an act of love not domination. It will be a spiritual presence, but no less real than the Spirit of the incarnation. You may like to note in passing how Fra Lippo Lippi draws on the physics of his time in showing the strange spheres of motion of the Spirit dove, and the light rays reaching out from Mary to it – a spiritual presence but a totally real one.*

We too can look for the signs of the Spirit at work in and around us in both spiritual and physical ways. Start watching out for them now, and as you think you discern them, record them and ponder them, just as Mary did.

From the overshadowing
Of Thy gold and silver wing
Shed on us, who to Thee sing,
Holy, heavenly Love.

Christopher Wordsworth
(from the hymn GRACIOUS SPIRIT HOLY GHOST) *

FRIDAY
The Visitation

Luke 1.39-55

At that time Mary got ready and hurried to a town in the hill country of Judea, where she entered Zechariah's home and greeted Elizabeth. When Elizabeth heard Mary's greeting, the baby leaped in her womb, and Elizabeth was filled with the Holy Spirit. In a loud voice she exclaimed: 'Blessed are you among women, and blessed is the child you will bear! But why am I so favoured, that the mother of my Lord should come to me? As soon as the sound of your greeting reached my ears, the baby in my womb leaped for joy. Blessed is she who has believed that what the Lord has said to her will be accomplished!'

Albertinelli, *The Visitation*

And Mary said: 'My soul glorifies the Lord and my spirit rejoices in God my Saviour, for he has been mindful of the humble state of his servant. From now on all generations will call me blessed, for the Mighty One has done great things for me – holy is his name. His mercy extends to those who fear him, from generation to generation. He has performed mighty deeds with his arm; he has scattered those who are proud in their inmost thoughts. He has brought down rulers from their thrones but has lifted up the humble. He has filled the hungry with good things but has sent the rich away empty. He has helped his servant Israel, remembering to be merciful to Abraham and his descendants forever, even as he said to our fathers.'

Now here is a real Magnificat moment! Two women meet who are united in the knowledge of a secret work of God's grace in their lives, in the private world of their pregnancy. The picture by Albertinelli speaks to me, in its leaning touch and enclosing arch, of the intimacy and mutuality of that meeting.

A friend of mine used to talk of 'bubbles of joy', and I can remember those strange times of secret joy, often tinged with apprehension, in my own life, when I have known for instance of a new but unannounced job, or a new creative project that is just taking shape.

A doctor, John Rose, in the patch of Cumbria where I work, wrote up his autobiography and told of a time when as a young man he was walking in the Alps and became detached from his friends.* Missing the last valley train home, he became overcome with cold and exhaustion, and was just ready to lie down and give up when another walker appeared, encouraging and helping him until the hotel was in sight. No word was said, and the walker was gone as strangely as he appeared. Rose told no one for a long time, but knew that God had met with him and saved him, and he carried the inspiration of that in his heart as long as he lived.

Perhaps you could start to keep a log-book now of your own walk with God, if you don't already do so. It can be quite private, a place for both your bubbles of joy and your questions of concern. You could share it from time to time with a trusted friend, but even if it stays completely secret, your journey will still not be alone.

In the stillness of the night
when the world was asleep
the almighty Word leapt out.
He came to Mary, He came to us;
Christ came to the land of Galilee.
Christ our Lord and our King.
O what a gift, what a wonderful gift
Who can tell the wonders of the Lord?
Let us open our eyes, our ears, and our hearts
It is Christ the Lord, it is He!

from Pat Uhl Howard, CANTICLE OF THE GIFT *

SATURDAY
The Nativity

Luke 2.1-21

In those days Caesar Augustus issued a decree that a census should be taken of the entire Roman world. (This was the first census that took place while Quirinius was governor of Syria.) And everyone went to his own town to register.

So Joseph also went up from the town of Nazareth in Galilee to Judea, to Bethlehem the town of David, because he belonged to the house and line of David. He went there to register with Mary, who was pledged to be married to him and was expecting a child. While they were there, the time came for the baby to be born, and she gave birth to her firstborn, a son. She wrapped him in cloths and placed him in a manger, because there was no room for them in the inn.

And there were shepherds living out in the fields nearby, keeping watch over their flocks at night. An angel of the Lord appeared to them, and the glory of the Lord shone around them, and they were terrified. But the angel said to them, 'Do not be afraid. I bring you good news of great joy that will be for all the people. Today in the town of David a Saviour has been born to you; he is Christ the Lord. This will be a sign to you: You will find a baby wrapped in cloths and lying in a manger.'

Suddenly a great company of the heavenly host appeared with the angel, praising God and saying, 'Glory to God in the highest, and on earth peace to men on whom his favour rests.'

When the angels had left them and gone into heaven, the shepherds said to one another, 'Let's go to Bethlehem and see this thing that has happened, which the Lord has told us about.'

So they hurried off and found Mary and Joseph, and the baby, who was lying in the manger. When they had seen him, they spread the word concerning what had been told them about this child, and all who heard it were amazed at what the shepherds said to them. But Mary treasured up all these things and pondered them in her heart. The shepherds returned, glorifying and praising God for all the things they had heard and seen, which were just as they had been told.

On the eighth day, when it was time to circumcise him, he was named Jesus, the name the angel had given him before he had been conceived.

'When the angels had left.' This is often the Gospel reading for the Sunday after Christmas, and always speaks to me of the emptiness that can follow a time of great excitement or celebration. It doesn't, of course, have to be like that. But in that case we have to take some responsibility for the matter. The shepherds, for instance, up sticks and go to see what it is all about.

In the same way we are going to need to find a willingness, sparked and spurred by our meeting with God, to stay with the story as Lent goes on, if we are going to make the most of our journey. One of the gifts of Lent is that it gives us a built-in framework for keeping going over a longer haul than we often manage.

A time to resolve, then, in the last of these opening and preparatory days, to 'go for gold' this Lent, like the Olympic athletes I am watching as I write this. You don't have to be a Class A saint. Remember that we are dealing with people like shepherds (not a trustworthy lot in Bible times) ... and us. The amazing action of the birth is all mixed up with the rough and readiness of life. Incidentally, if you ever get the chance to see the 'Second Shepherds' Play'* in the Wakefield Mystery Play cycle, seize it, and laugh 'til you split at the Holy Nativity embedded in the mediaeval equivalent of *Only Fools and Horses*, and all without disrespect.

So let's get going – unlike the rather sceptical and footsore Joseph in this extract from della Francesca's painting of *The Nativity* (below), who seems far from ready for the road ahead.

Lord, I can sympathise with Joseph:
Life's road is hard,
And sometimes my feet hurt too.
But when I walked a country lane
And complained about it all to you,
I looked down at the stony path
And remembered your road to Calvary.

della Francesca, *The Nativity* (detail)

WEEK 1 # STUDY MATERIAL

 If you are in a group, spend some time just getting to know each other or catching up. Then think a bit together or on your own about times when you have received unexpected news (happy or sad), and entered into a time of waiting as a result. Some of the times may be painful to remember (news of an illness ...), so support each other in your listening, or seek out a friend to share them with if you are studying on your own, if you need to.

Look at the account of the Annunciation in Luke 1.26-38 (Thursday's passage). Read it through carefully. Identify the different thoughts and feelings that you see in Mary, and relate them to the ones you have had yourself. Does it feel the same or different? Which do you think was the most significant for her? Which for you?

Imagine yourself in the scene. You are Mary, reading the scriptures perhaps. You sense a presence ... Listen for what God may be saying not only to Mary but to you.

 Spend some time in intercession for people that you know who have received news, and for people who are in a time of waiting.

Picture the Holy Spirit hovering over them like a dove, present with them in their sorrows and joys. Commend them to the care of God – but be aware of any prompting from God as to ways you can help too.

Many of the suggestions for study will be helped if you can gather together some colour reproductions of paintings of the Bible scenes to which they refer. The internet is a good source of these (and some references are given in the list of illustrations) but be aware of any copyright restrictions that apply.

SUNDAY (First Sunday of Lent)
THE CALL OF CHRIST

 Boots on! I hope you're ready for the off, now; ready for the action, for the story of your Lent. This first full week of studies focuses on our calling, by looking at the calling and sending of the first disciples. They faced some radical choices. We in our turn must face some radical questions.

It's a matter of the boot camp. Unless we get the basics, the beginnings, the training right, then the whole journey will be at risk.

We need to prepare ourselves amongst other things for the spiritual challenges that the journey will bring us. The theme of the scripture readings in some churches this Sunday will be the Temptation of Christ. We can look and wonder and learn from how even he didn't just sail majestically into ministry, but had to get the foundations right and make sure that he was within God's will.

So start to listen today for the voice of God, the voice that calls, that heals, that keeps us safely on the path and strengthens us when we find the going tough.

Almighty God,
whose Son Jesus Christ fasted forty days in the wilderness,
and was tempted as we are, yet without sin:
give us grace to discipline ourselves in obedience to your Spirit;
and, as you know our weakness,
so may we know your power to save;
through Jesus Christ your Son our Lord,
who is alive and reigns with you,
in the unity of the Holy Spirit,
one God, now and for ever.

COMMON WORSHIP, Collect for First Sunday of Lent *

WEEK 2 MONDAY
The Call of the Disciples

Luke 5.1-11

One day as Jesus was standing by the Lake of Gennesaret, with the people crowding around him and listening to the word of God, he saw at the water's edge two boats, left there by the fishermen, who were washing their nets. He got into one of the boats, the one belonging to Simon, and asked him to put out a little from shore. Then he sat down and taught the people from the boat.

When he had finished speaking, he said to Simon, 'Put out into deep water, and let down the nets for a catch.'

Simon answered, 'Master, we've worked hard all night and haven't caught anything. But because you say so, I will let down the nets.'

When they had done so, they caught such a large number of fish that their nets began to break. So they signalled their partners in the other boat to come and help them, and they came and filled both boats so full that they began to sink.

When Simon Peter saw this, he fell at Jesus' knees and said, 'Go away from me, Lord; I am a sinful man!' For he and all his companions were astonished at the catch of fish they had taken, and so were James and John, the sons of Zebedee, Simon's partners.

Then Jesus said to Simon, 'Don't be afraid; from now on you will catch men.' So they pulled their boats up on shore, left everything and followed him.

Bassano's painting of *The Miraculous Draught* is a swirl of red and orange, green and blue. In the background the very workaday business is going on of getting the catch in. But leaping from it is a scene of revelation and worship, as Peter falls before Christ as Lord.

Today's passage is shot through with the same contrast. On the one hand Jesus is amongst men who must have known him, and possibly known him well. These were not large communities. On the other hand, 'one day', into this normality breaks the quite

Bassano,
*The
Miraculous
Draught
of Fishes*

exceptional. A boat is borrowed, there is some talking and listening, and then the unexpected suggestion to put out again for fish, and its amazing consequence.

All the gospels have some version of the story. It had an obvious application to evangelism for the early church. But it speaks to me too of the simple historical shock of the carpenter-turned-teacher flabbergasting his fisherman friends, first with an unlikely suggestion, then with an even more unlikely result.

Heaven in ordinary. This is the incarnation in miniature, God breaking in against all expectations to the daily routine of our lives. It was enough to turn the fishermen into fishers of men, to start the movement that would change the world, and a golden chain of faith whose other end reaches to us. It was not meant as just a beginning. I for one, and millions more, have found this same in-breaking into my life that left nothing the same. Are you ready for it too?

O Most Merciful Redeemer,
Friend and Brother;
May I know Thee more clearly,
Love Thee more dearly,
And follow Thee more nearly,
Day by day.
St Richard of Chichester *

TUESDAY
The Call of Levi

Luke 5.27-32

After this, Jesus went out and saw a tax collector by the name of Levi sitting at his tax booth. 'Follow me,' Jesus said to him, and Levi got up, left everything and followed him.

Then Levi held a great banquet for Jesus at his house, and a large crowd of tax collectors and others were eating with them. But the Pharisees and the teachers of the law who belonged to their sect complained to his disciples, 'Why do you eat and drink with tax collectors and 'sinners'?'

Jesus answered them, 'It is not the healthy who need a doctor, but the sick. I have not come to call the righteous, but sinners to repentance.'

Caravaggio,
*The Call of
Matthew*
(detail)

The fishermen-disciples may have been a rough and ready lot, but they were more or less within the pale. Not so this collector of taxes! Caravaggio (whose own life was outrageous enough) loved to create an atmosphere in his paintings, with dark shadows, moody lighting and dramatic gestures. This was a scene he could not resist. The booth has become a gangster-like back room, and Christ points across the table like Banquo's ghost. There is a confusion of arms, but at the far left Levi or Matthew slumps with his head in his hands, a young man overtaken and overwhelmed, and in the throes of conversion.

He is being turned inside out. This alien group of disciples is about to become his new in-group. But there is more inside-outness going on than that. The disciple group is both radically 'in' and radically 'out' of the society around it. It is the breaking in and foundation of the kingdom that Israel was always meant to be.* But it attracts the rejected and is met with rejection.

Most of us are fairly sensitive to the atmospheres of being 'in' and 'out'. And many of us bear substantial scars of rejection, which can be surprisingly difficult to heal properly, perhaps because the hurt is so deep and the scar tissue so defensive a covering.

Part of the ministry of Jesus then and now is to offer us the possibility of such a delicate healing. If we can move on from Matthew/Levi's position in the painting, which speaks so eloquently of self-pity and despair, and like him dare to walk with Christ, there is a new life there for us to find too.

Only remember: the new life is not the old life with all the nasty bits taken out, with us basking in affirmation and love at its centre. It is about being with Jesus, not only in the heights but in the depths of the world, and that will mean sharing in his suffering and rejection as well as his presence and Spirit. It is a matter of both a heavenly Trans-figuration and a very earthly Transformation, as we shall shortly see.

Hear what comfortable words our Saviour Christ saith unto all that truly turn to him.
Come unto me all that travail and are heavy laden, and I will refresh you.
St Matthew 11.28 (AUTHORISED VERSION)

WEDNESDAY
The Twelve

WEEK 2

Luke 6.12-16

One of those days Jesus went out to a mountainside to pray, and spent the night praying to God. When morning came, he called his disciples to him and chose twelve of them, whom he also designated apostles: Simon (whom he named Peter), his brother Andrew, James, John, Philip, Bartholomew, Matthew, Thomas, James son of Alphaeus, Simon who was called the Zealot, Judas son of James, and Judas Iscariot, who became a traitor.

'Twelve' had something of the same resonance in Bible times as 'Eleven' does today – as in 'The England Eleven' for the Test Match. What Jesus is doing is picking 'The Israel Twelve', one apostle for each tribe, a symbol of a new foundation of the twelve tribes of Israel, God's people.

Unsurprisingly, this was for Jesus a matter of much prayer. Part of my own work is helping choose ministers of one sort and another, and if the weight of responsibility I feel in the shallow waters I have to negotiate is anything to go by, Jesus' sense of responsibility here must have been immense.

No wonder he spends the night in prayer to God, seeking as we read elsewhere to align his will with God's, so that he is doing only what the Father is doing, so that God's will is done and God's kingdom can come. Pleasing himself, the disciples, or indeed the people, was simply not the agenda.

What remains much more surprising is the Twelve who were called. As I write, our local team (Carlisle United) has been relegated from the Football League, and Jesus' choice of the disciples is as if Carlisle had been chosen en bloc to represent England in the European finals. I doubt that as a football manager 'Jesus Josephson' would have lasted a week.

In a good side though, as Chelsea's new manager is telling us, what matters is not so much individual talent as whether the players share the manager's vision and are committed to playing as a team.

And here the first followers of Jesus have a chance. One of the commentators' theories about the Twelve is that they were envisaged as the crew of a twelve-oar boat, seated in pairs. That has to be speculation, but what is certain is that Galilean fishermen, rugged and competitive individuals though they were, were well used to the partnership and teamwork of rowing together and getting the catch in.

So put together Simon Peter's readiness to follow Jesus' instruction, James and John's willingness to give up everything and follow him, Levi's life-changing commitment – and you have the sort of team God needs.

Time then to ask ourselves, in this individualistic age, how ready we are to throw in our lot with the Christians around us, and how ready too to exchange our post-modern detachment for commitment to Christ and the will of God.

The future of the church, like its foundation, lies in a willingness for its leaders and members too to be radically in community with each other, and radically committed to going God's way, however counter-cultural that is. Not the easiest of programmes for the typical C of E parishes I know and love!

O God, who hast bound us together in this bundle of life,
give us grace to understand how our lives depend upon the courage,
the industry, the honesty and the integrity of our fellow men:
that we may be mindful of their needs and grateful for their faithfulness,
and faithful in our responsibilities to them, through Jesus Christ our Lord.

Reinhold Niebuhr *

WEEK 2 THURSDAY
Sent Out

Luke 9.1-9

When Jesus had called the Twelve together, he gave them power and authority to drive out all demons and to cure diseases, and he sent them out to preach the kingdom of God and to heal the sick. He told them: 'Take nothing for the journey – no staff, no bag, no bread, no money, no extra tunic. Whatever house you enter, stay there until you leave that town. If people do not welcome you, shake the dust off your feet when you leave their town, as a testimony against them.' So they set out and went from village to village, preaching the gospel and healing people everywhere.

Now Herod the tetrarch heard about all that was going on. And he was perplexed, because some were saying that John had been raised from the dead, others that Elijah had appeared, and still others that one of the prophets of long ago had come back to life. But Herod said, 'I beheaded John. Who, then, is this I hear such things about?' And he tried to see him.

From calling to sending ... First Jesus calls his apostles. Then he shows them in word and deed what their mission is. In Luke's Gospel, the choosing of the Twelve is followed by the keynote teaching block of the 'Sermon on the Plain' and a series of high-profile miracles – the healing of the Centurion's servant, the raising of the widow's son and Jairus' daughter, the stilling of the storm – which give substance to Jesus' answer to John the Baptist's question, 'Are you the one?', the underlying theme of this section of Luke's gospel.

Then Jesus sends the apostles out to share in the mission themselves. We live in a world of ever-increasing training and regulation, authorisation and qualification. It is refreshing to see a simpler, apprenticeship, learning-by-doing methodology in action.

As we consider our own ministry, and call and prepare others for it in our churches, there is perhaps something for us to learn here.

As I look back on my own ministry I know that I have faced the temptation to spend far too long in the library before getting out into the garden, as a kindly but keen-spirited counsellor once put it, and discover his call to me in a new way. I also see many people in our churches (and I write as someone who was once an education professional) who experience our selection and training systems as a barrier, or who train for years for one ministry only to find that their calling is really to another when they finally start to practise it. Three cheers for the new schemes of locally licensed and commissioned ministry that give people a chance to discover and explore their gifts before going on to fuller training.

Our concern now, though, is not with such structural issues but with our own following of Christ. Is there some aspect of ministry or piece of action that we are avoiding getting round to, and why? How does what we are doing measure up to the basic kingdom agenda given to these first disciples? If we are frustrated, as so many are, that we are locked into maintenance and barely getting going in mission, is it time to risk setting out and doing the new thing, even if some of the old is still stuck in place? If the new thing really is the work of God as begun by Christ and passed on to the apostles and to us, then we probably should have started on it long ago, but better late than never!

Sometimes, Lord,
I just have to 'do it'.
All that training,
All that thinking …
All that worrying,
All that fear …
Then when I make the visit,
Face up to the conversation,
Broach the dreaded subject,
I find you are there already
And the problem
Was me.

WEEK 2 FRIDAY
At Caesarea Philippi

Luke 9.18-27

Once when Jesus was praying in private and his disciples were with him, he asked them, 'Who do the crowds say I am?'

They replied, 'Some say John the Baptist; others say Elijah; and still others, that one of the prophets of long ago has come back to life.'

'But what about you?' he asked. 'Who do you say I am?'

Peter answered, 'The Christ of God.'

Jesus strictly warned them not to tell this to anyone. And he said, 'The Son of Man must suffer many things and be rejected by the elders, chief priests and teachers of the law, and he must be killed and on the third day be raised to life.'

Then he said to them all: 'If anyone would come after me, he must deny himself and take up his cross daily and follow me. For whoever wants to save his life will lose it, but whoever loses his life for me will save it. What good is it for a man to gain the whole world, and yet lose or forfeit his very self? If anyone is ashamed of me and my words, the Son of Man will be ashamed of him when he comes in his glory and in the glory of the Father and of the holy angels. I tell you the truth, some who are standing here will not taste death before they see the kingdom of God.'

Who, then, do I say that he is? It's true that 'sometimes I just have to do it', as we prayed yesterday. But only as long as I am aware enough of God and his will to be in tune with him.

So Jesus takes the disciples away privately to check out the basics. Have they really understood who he is, and what this mission is all about? He chooses to take them (according to Matthew and Mark) to Caesarea Philippi, in the far north of the country under the slopes of Mount Hermon, a sort of first-century Lucknow for soldiers and the like on furlough. An unlikely place for the band of apostles, especially as it was centred on a shrine to Pan!

Tissot, *The Confession of Peter*

Tissot's rather romantic watercolour of the scene has Peter literally scratching his head as he tries to work it all out. It captures the externals of the scenery well, but not perhaps the internal tension. This is a crucial moment, the turning point of Luke's Gospel. Peter's confession will be followed immediately by the prediction of the Passion and teaching on the cost of discipleship. The stakes could not be higher.

What times can you make to come together around Christ with your own fellow-worshippers and fellow-workers and check out again the basics of your call?

Suddenly, Lord,
it's getting very serious.
Like the TA soldier
When the call-up papers arrive.
That's when I discover
Who I really think you are:
And who I really am.

WEEK 2: *The Call of Christ*   **21**

WEEK 2 SATURDAY
The Transfiguration

Raphael, *The Transfiguration*

Luke 9:28-45

About eight days after Jesus said this, he took Peter, John and James with him and went up onto a mountain to pray. As he was praying, the appearance of his face changed, and his clothes became as bright as a flash of lightning. Two men, Moses and Elijah, appeared in glorious splendour, talking with Jesus. They spoke about his departure, which he was about to bring to fulfilment at Jerusalem. Peter and his companions were very sleepy, but when they became fully awake, they saw his glory and the two men standing with him. As the men were leaving Jesus, Peter said to him, 'Master, it is good for us to be here. Let us put up three shelters – one for you, one for Moses and one for Elijah.' (He did not know what he was saying.)

While he was speaking, a cloud appeared and enveloped them, and they were afraid as they entered the cloud. A voice came from the cloud, saying, 'This is my Son, whom I have chosen; listen to him.' When the voice had spoken, they found that Jesus was alone. The disciples kept this to themselves, and told no one at that time what they had seen.

The next day, when they came down from the mountain, a large crowd met him. A man in the crowd called out, 'Teacher, I beg you to look at my son, for he is my only child. A spirit seizes him and he suddenly screams; it throws him into convulsions so that he foams at the mouth. It scarcely ever leaves him and is destroying him. I begged your disciples to drive it out, but they could not.'

'O unbelieving and perverse generation,' Jesus replied, 'how long shall I stay with you and put up with you? Bring your son here.'

Even while the boy was coming, the demon threw him to the ground in a convulsion. But Jesus rebuked the evil spirit, healed the boy and gave him back to his father. And they were all amazed at the greatness of God.

While everyone was marvelling at all that Jesus did, he said to his disciples, 'Listen carefully to what I am about to tell you: The Son of Man is going to be betrayed into the hands of men.' But they did not understand what this meant. It was hidden from them, so that they did not grasp it, and they were afraid to ask him about it.

Peter has taken a risk and declared his faith in Jesus as Messiah. So often it's when we do that that the door is opened for God to respond, and we find ourselves wonderfully encouraged in our calling and in our lives.

Transfiguration – and then the work of Transformation begins. In Raphael's famous painting of today's scene, and very unusually, these two themes are set alongside each other. Above is Christ on the mountain; Moses and Elijah alongside him; Peter, James and John overcome. Below, the other disciples try in vain to heal the boy with an evil spirit. The Old Law (see the book in the bottom left corner) is getting them nowhere. A flurry of arms leads us first to the boy and then up to Jesus: only he – and those in whom his work continues – can make a difference.

Looking back over the week we can see a to-and-fro movement which began in our open-ness to God's call and our willingness to accept his touch on our lives. This can lead to a re-making of our commitment to one another and the kingdom and our taking the risk of making a start on its work. Further reflection and renewed commitment find affirmation from God and a new sending out to engage in his mission.

We're on the way! It will always be an accompanied journey with Christ in us and among us, and the stories will be good ones!

Christ has no body now on earth but yours, no hands but yours, no feet but yours; yours are the eyes through which he is to look with compassion on the world; yours are the feet with which he is to go about doing good; and yours the hands with which he is to bless us now.

St Teresa of Avila *

Look back over the various aspects of the disciples' calling and sending that we have encountered this week. Which part of the story do you identify with the most? A sense of calling (with reluctance, with joy)? Surprise, guilt or unworthiness? Being part of a fellowship (love them, or hate them …)? Asked to do something (too much, or not enough)? Longing to be with Jesus? Or struggling to find him? Lost in rapture? Or just lost?

Have a look at the account of the conversation at Caesarea Philippi in Luke 9.18-27 (Friday's passage). 'Who do you say that I am?' Many of our questions resolve themselves when we re-focus our faith on Christ. Gather together some pictures of him of as many sorts as you can.

(CMS publish a useful collection called *The Christ we Share*,* and there have been several coffee-table books of images of Christ in fine art.) Which image helps you the most? Do any surprise or shock you? Why? Who is this man?

Place the candle where you can (all) see it. Read or remember the verse where Jesus says, 'I am the light of the world. Whoever follows me will never walk in darkness, but will have the light of life.' (John 8.12) Remember that Jesus is with you as you meet in his name, and pray that you will recognise that presence and know his light in your life, in whatever image you find him.

SUNDAY (Second Sunday of Lent)
STORIES ON THE WAY

WEEK 3

On the Way! I can't help comparing this pilgrim band with that of Chaucer's Canterbury Pilgrims* – a very mixed bag! (Us too …) Those pilgrims told stories to each other as they travelled, and so also Jesus tells stories: little stories which say something important about the big story that is going on; his story.

Rembrandt, *The Return of the Prodigal Son*

The lectionary themes this Sunday have to do with setting out on the way, amongst other things. Perhaps this is not a bad time to recollect our own stories of life and faith, and the stories of those who have encouraged us.

You could draw a time-line or map of your journey; look through old photos, books, notes that are its snail-trail; just remember in silence.

Give thanks, and remember that we are all part of God's great story. Just keep to the path!

Almighty God,
you show to those who are in error the light of your truth,
that they may return to the way of righteousness:
grant to all those who are admitted into the fellowship of Christ's religion,
that they may reject those things that are contrary to their profession,
and follow all such things as are agreeable to the same;
through our Lord Jesus Christ,
who is alive and reigns with you,
in the unity of the Holy Spirit,
one God, now and for ever.

COMMON WORSHIP, Collect for Second Sunday of Lent *

MONDAY
The Good Samaritan

Luke 10.25-37

On one occasion an expert in the law stood up to test Jesus. 'Teacher,' he asked, 'what must I do to inherit eternal life?'

'What is written in the Law?' he replied. 'How do you read it?'

He answered: "'Love the Lord your God with all your heart and with all your soul and with all your strength and with all your mind'; and, 'Love your neighbour as yourself.'"

'You have answered correctly,' Jesus replied. 'Do this and you will live.'

But he wanted to justify himself, so he asked Jesus, 'And who is my neighbour?'

Van Gogh,
*The Good
Samaritan*

In reply Jesus said: 'A man was going down from Jerusalem to Jericho, when he fell into the hands of robbers. They stripped him of his clothes, beat him and went away, leaving him half dead. A priest happened to be going down the same road, and when he saw the man, he passed by on the other side. So too, a Levite, when he came to the place and saw him, passed by on the other side. But a Samaritan, as he travelled, came where the man was; and when he saw him, he took pity on him. He went to him and bandaged his wounds, pouring on oil and wine. Then he put the man on his own donkey, took him to an inn and took care of him. The next day he took out two silver coins and gave them to the innkeeper. "Look after him," he said, "and when I return, I will reimburse you for any extra expense you may have."

'Which of these three do you think was a neighbour to the man who fell into the hands of robbers?'

The expert in the law replied, 'The one who had mercy on him.'

Jesus told him, 'Go and do likewise.'

This is not a comfortable story for any clerics who have found themselves rushing from one duty to the next, and missing the real need along the way. The lawyer would have known he was bound in duty and charity to his fellow Jews: his horizon is radically expanded by Jesus to include all his neighbours. We in the Christian Church can easily become over-preoccupied by our fellowships, and forget that they are there for the sake of the world, not to escape from it.

Good Lenten discipline involves taking things up and looking outwards, as well as giving things up and looking within. You could start to reflect on that now.

The story has another dimension, though: the victim, who is easily forgotten because his role is so passive. Van Gogh's painting of the story (made when he himself was confined because of illness) brings home the pained mass of his body, still in the midst of the swirling brush-strokes of the vivid, newly-available, synthetic colours, and Samaritan and victim together seem to prefigure the Cross, where Christ too is both victim and pain-bearer.

The Samaritan's treatment of the man's wounds was medically sensible and totally compassionate: but I don't suppose that made them sting any the less. As we try to re-orientate ourselves towards God, travel along his way, we too may need some treatment. Most of us carry wounds, and it is as natural to resist the probing touch of the healer as it is to shy away from the dentist's drill. But they still do need cleaning out and renewing. And we need a healer who can help us bear the pain.

It would make a good sign in a hospital, amongst all the others, outside the chapel: 'To the Pain-Bearer'.* If all the talk of moving on feels a bit too much – perhaps you need to spend some time quietly there now and know that you are held by God.

Hold me Lord
When I can't stand any longer,
When I'm taking myself for dead,
When the bubble of life has burst.
Let me hide myself
In you.

TUESDAY
The Rich Fool

Luke 12.13-21

Someone in the crowd said to him, 'Teacher, tell my brother to divide the inheritance with me.'

Jesus replied, 'Man, who appointed me a judge or an arbiter between you?' Then he said to them, 'Watch out! Be on your guard against all kinds of greed; a man's life does not consist in the abundance of his possessions.'

And he told them this parable: 'The ground of a certain rich man produced a good crop. He thought to himself, 'What shall I do? I have no place to store my crops.'

'Then he said, 'This is what I'll do. I will tear down my barns and build bigger ones, and there I will store all my grain and my goods. And I'll say to myself, 'You have plenty of good things laid up for many years. Take life easy; eat, drink and be merry.''

'But God said to him, 'You fool! This very night your life will be demanded from you. Then who will get what you have prepared for yourself?'

'This is how it will be with anyone who stores up things for himself but is not rich toward God.'

We've been thinking a bit about being held by God, and that's good and right. One of Luke's themes, though, is that we are called as human beings to take responsibility for our lives and our actions. We will see it come out in the Passion narrative (remember how Jesus throws the words back at his interrogators: 'That is what you say').

Here – and every counsellor and spiritual director, parent and teacher has encountered it – a man tries to manipulate Jesus onto his side in a family squabble, so that he can hide behind Jesus' authority. What he needs to do is enter into a properly adult negotiation with his brother to sort things out. I say 'adult' because there is a certain childishness involved in the man's attitude; and while it can be fun for adults to play in a childlike way together (lovers do it all the time) there is nothing but trouble in store when adults start crossing the wires and becoming either all childish or all parental towards each other. If you want to explore the idea more, look out for Eric Berne's classic book, *Games People Play*,* and you'll find it all there.

The rich man in the story that follows is being child**ish** in another way too. We call it child-**like** innocently to fail to realise the consequences of our actions, and even just to see things from our point of view. But we say childish when one who is able to take a bigger view does not do so; childish, and selfish too.

Most of Jesus' hearers, we can speculate, were not possessed of either barns or riches, so the man in the story would be a natural scapegoat for them. Jesus, though, is not simply knocking the rich and siding with the poor. He is challenging both alike to be 'rich toward God'. What does that mean?

God has just stepped into the story – rather unusually – in the first person, and his purpose is to call 'Time' on the man's life and bring in the final accounting. So the one who is rich towards God is the one whom God will deem worthy for heaven – and we know from elsewhere that this is not at all a matter of money but of costly trust and faithful action.

Riches and belongings can become an insulation against ultimate realities. So can the scar tissue we build up round our wounds. There comes a time when we have to not just be held by God but be ready to act, in another kind of dependence. If our feet get sore, we will find his hospitality and healing on the way.

 Frankly, Lord, it was easier when we had less.
I didn't believe it at the time,
But now we've got more money, more status …
Teach me Lord
Still to depend on you
And build your kingdom
Not bigger barns for me,
Fool that I am.

WEEK 3

WEDNESDAY
The Great Banquet

Luke 14.15-24

When one of those at the table with him heard this, he said to Jesus, 'Blessed is the man who will eat at the feast in the kingdom of God.'

Jesus replied: 'A certain man was preparing a great banquet and invited many guests. At the time of the banquet he sent his servant to tell those who had been invited, "Come, for everything is now ready."

'But they all alike began to make excuses. The first said, "I have just bought a field, and I must go and see it. Please excuse me."

'Another said, "I have just bought five yoke of oxen, and I'm on my way to try them out. Please excuse me."

'Still another said, "I just got married, so I can't come."

'The servant came back and reported this to his master. Then the owner of the house became angry and ordered his servant, "Go out quickly into the streets and alleys of the town and bring in the poor, the crippled, the blind and the lame."

'"Sir," the servant said, "what you ordered has been done, but there is still room."

'Then the master told his servant, "Go out to the roads and country lanes and make them come in, so that my house will be full. I tell you, not one of those men who were invited will get a taste of my banquet."'

The 'Jesus Mafa' picture from Africa captures beautifully the compassion of the master as he welcomes in the lame and poor. There is hope here for the footsore on the Way. As Jesus preached the kingdom he surely offered real hope and blessing to the poor – spiritually real in its foundations, but credibly real in physical terms too. The new way of living was beginning now!

But there is a massive warning too. Either side of the welcomed poor stand a group of people whose fate is far less pleasant. Here, those

who profess a relationship with the master of the banquet, but find every excuse not to do anything about it. There, other poor who are also resistant to the invitation, but are compelled to come. I have awkward memories of baptism Sundays in the parish church when the regulars stayed away and the pews were filled with highly scrubbed chaps who were obviously wanting to be somewhere else ...

A vicar's wrath more easily descends on the first group, and the parable as originally told must have fallen hard on the ears of pious Jews. I am intrigued, though, by the second group, those compelled to come in.

I don't want to write off this coda to the story as an addition, nor spiritualise it into a sort of prediction that there are still people out there for us to evangelize.

I want rather to go back to my uncomfortable chaps in the pews. A few of them were genuine villains, and we played an undeclared game of I-know-that-you-know, of preaching and pretending. They are not likely guests at the banquet. But most were simply uncomfortably off their patch, and there because of the compulsion of love – for their child, their family, their friends. This is a sort of compulsion that we can live with, in fact that we all need, I and you and they together.

Most merciful Lord, your love compels us to come in. Our hands were unclean, our hearts were unprepared; we were not fit even to eat the crumbs from under your table. But you, Lord, are the God of our salvation, and share your bread with sinners. So cleanse and feed us with the precious body and blood of your Son, that he may live in us and we in him; and that we, with the whole company of Christ, may sit and eat in your kingdom.

COMMON WORSHIP, alternative Prayer of Humble Access *

THURSDAY
The Lost Son

Luke 15.11-32

Jesus continued: 'There was a man who had two sons. The younger one said to his father, "Father, give me my share of the estate." So he divided his property between them.

'Not long after that, the younger son got together all he had, set off for a distant country and there squandered his wealth in wild living. After he had spent everything, there was a severe famine in that whole country, and he began to be in need. So he went and hired himself out to a citizen of that country, who sent him to his fields to feed pigs. He longed to fill his stomach with the pods that the pigs were eating, but no one gave him anything.

'When he came to his senses, he said, "How many of my father's hired men have food to spare, and here I am starving to death! I will set out and go back to my father and say to him: Father, I have sinned against heaven and against you. I am no longer worthy to be called your son; make me like one of your hired men." So he got up and went to his father.

'But while he was still a long way off, his father saw him and was filled with compassion for him; he ran to his son, threw his arms around him and kissed him. 'The son said to him, "Father, I have sinned against heaven and against you. I am no longer worthy to be called your son."

'But the father said to his servants, "Quick! Bring the best robe and put it on him. Put a ring on his finger and sandals on his feet. Bring the fattened calf and kill it. Let's have a feast and celebrate. For this son of mine was dead and is alive again; he was lost and is found." So they began to celebrate.

'Meanwhile, the older son was in the field. When he came near the house, he heard music and dancing. So he called one of the servants and asked him what was going on. 'Your brother has come,' he replied, 'and your father has killed the fattened calf because he has him back safe and sound.'

'The older brother became angry and refused to go in. So his father went out and pleaded with him. But he answered his father, "Look! All these years I've been slaving for you and never disobeyed your orders. Yet you never gave me even a young goat so I could celebrate with my friends. But when this son of yours who has squandered your property with prostitutes comes home, you kill the fattened calf for him!"

'"My son," the father said, "you are always with me, and everything I have is yours. But we had to celebrate and be glad, because this brother of yours was dead and is alive again; he was lost and is found."'

This is a story that is lodged deep in our psyche – a story that speaks of redemption itself, the journey of every prodigal, every soul back to God.

Rembrandt's painting is also not easily forgotten. The lost son is restored to the bosom of his father, simultaneously child and prematurely aged by experience. And is that the elder brother who looks on so emptily, so wanly from behind? This restoration is a closed book to him. He is becoming a creature of the shades in his sullen self-pity.

The sad thing is that one generation's redeemed prodigals so easily become the next's elder brothers. We as the church ought to be forever at the heart of the celebration, but how many 'celebrations of Holy Communion', for instance, live up to the name?

The answer lies with each one of us. Every day, every service, can, if we will let it, be a prodigal's return.

Father of all, we give you thanks and praise, that when we were still far off you met us in your Son and brought us home. Dying and living, he declared your love, gave us grace, and opened the gate of glory. May we who share Christ's body live his risen life; we who drink his cup bring life to others; we whom the Spirit lights give light to the world. Keep us firm in the hope you have set before us, so we and all your children shall be free, and the whole earth live to praise your name; through Jesus Christ our Lord. Amen.

COMMON WORSHIP, Post-communion prayer *

FRIDAY
The Shrewd Manager

German woodcut, *The Shrewd Manager*

Luke 16.1-15

Jesus told his disciples: There was a rich man whose manager was accused of wasting his possessions. So he called him in and asked him, "What is this I hear about you? Give an account of your management, because you cannot be manager any longer."

'The manager said to himself, "What shall I do now? My master is taking away my job. I'm not strong enough to dig, and I'm ashamed to beg – I know what I'll do so that, when I lose my job here, people will welcome me into their houses."

'So he called in each one of his master's debtors. He asked the first, "How much do you owe my master?"

'"Eight hundred gallons of olive oil," he replied.

'The manager told him, "Take your bill, sit down quickly, and make it four hundred."

'Then he asked the second, "And how much do you owe?"

'"A thousand bushels of wheat," he replied.

'He told him, "Take your bill and make it eight hundred."

'The master commended the dishonest manager because he had acted shrewdly. For the people of this world are more shrewd in dealing with their own kind than are the people of the light. I tell you, use worldly wealth to gain friends for yourselves, so that when it is gone, you will be welcomed into eternal dwellings.

'Whoever can be trusted with very little can also be trusted with much, and whoever is dishonest with very little will also be dishonest with much. So if you have not been trustworthy in handling worldly wealth, who will trust you with true riches? And if you have not been trustworthy with someone else's property, who will give you property of your own?

'No servant can serve two masters. Either he will hate the one and love the other, or he will be devoted to the one and despise the other. You cannot serve both God and Money.'

The Pharisees, who loved money, heard all this and were sneering at Jesus. He said to them, 'You are the ones who justify yourselves in the eyes of men, but God knows your hearts. What is highly valued among men is detestable in God's sight.

Unsurprisingly, Jesus' stories are very Jewish in their style and reference. The kingdom banquet, judges and Samaritans – and now one that only makes sense when we understand that lending money at interest was forbidden under Jewish law, and that the way folk got round this was by pretending that a larger sum had been lent than really was. The steward reduces the amount on the bill back to the actual debt. Any challenge to his actions would reveal the sharp – if common enough – practice of his master. That, at least, is one very respectable interpretation of what is going on.

So what is the point of the story? As delivered by Jesus, it is that the disciples (to whom the story is being told) should not hang on to their money but use it in ways which will make us welcome both in the homes around us and in our eternal home.

These ways may not be the ones we would expect! There is a little of the shrewd manager in Jesus: the divine love he incarnates is profligate and he forgives debts (sins) in a way that many said he was not entitled to do. I wonder how choosy we are about the style and environment in which we work out our redemption.

Be ready, then, for your Way to lead you into unexpected, even uncongenial places; to do out-of-character and profligate things; as long as it is all within God's will.

*Lord, help us to live this day quietly, easily; to lean upon
Thy great strength trustfully, peacefully; to wait for the unfolding
of Thy will patiently, joyously; to face the future confidently,
courageously.*

St Francis of Assisi *

The Rich Man and Lazarus

Luke 16.19-31

'There was a rich man who was dressed in purple and fine linen and lived in luxury every day. At his gate was laid a beggar named Lazarus, covered with sores and longing to eat what fell from the rich man's table. Even the dogs came and licked his sores.

'The time came when the beggar died and the angels carried him to Abraham's side. The rich man also died and was buried. In hell, where he was in torment, he looked up and saw Abraham far away, with Lazarus by his side. So he called to him, "Father Abraham, have pity on me and send Lazarus to dip the tip of his finger in water and cool my tongue, because I am in agony in this fire."

'But Abraham replied, "Son, remember that in your lifetime you received your good things, while Lazarus received bad things, but now he is comforted here and you are in agony. And besides all this, between us and you a great chasm has been fixed, so that those who want to go from here to you cannot, nor can anyone cross over from there to us."

'He answered, "Then I beg you, father, send Lazarus to my father's house, for I have five brothers. Let him warn them, so that they will not also come to this place of torment."

'Abraham replied, "They have Moses and the Prophets; let them listen to them."

'"No, father Abraham," he said, "but if someone from the dead goes to them, they will repent."

'He said to him, "If they do not listen to Moses and the Prophets, they will not be convinced even if someone rises from the dead."'

Our week of stories is nearly over. How are you finding them? They have a nasty habit of creeping under our guard and raising big questions, perhaps because we don't at first see ourselves in the story – or see ourselves as the faithful in it – and then …

Here is another thoroughly Jewish story, that seems well distant from our own world. We neither have beggars camped at our door, nor do we envisage the after-life in these pre-Christian terms. Time to open it up to us and us up to it.

Let's start with the rich man. He would naturally be a Sadducee – the establishment party if you like. Finding himself in hell would have been a big surprise, not only because he would probably have thought of himself as deserving better, but because as a Sadducee he didn't believe in this sort of after-life anyway.

Abraham says that the man's brothers have Moses and the Prophets to guide them because the written Torah was the only law the Sadducees acknowledged. They did not share the Pharisees' enthusiasm for applying it to daily life and hedging it round with a multiplicity of regulations, nor did they share the concern of the Essenes, for example, for holiness. An establishment faith indeed.

And now perhaps the application is starting to open up. To what extent have we ourselves learnt to see our daily living as accountable to God, lapsing neither into acting as if God were not, nor into an unhealthy and neurotic attention to detail? Scarily, we have indeed had one rise from the dead to show us the way – and still we may be as the rich man was: neither really seeing those in need around us (let alone helping them), nor really understanding the urgent relationship between that and the life to come.

Jerusalem is in sight – it is time to consider our position.

 O Lord, we beseech thee mercifully to receive the prayers of thy people which call upon thee; and grant that they may both perceive and know what things they ought to do, and also may have grace and power faithfully to fulfil the same; through Jesus Christ our Lord.

BOOK OF COMMON PRAYER, Collect for the First Sunday after Epiphany *

STUDY MATERIAL

Spend some time reflecting on how your Lenten journey is going. If it was a real journey, would you be making progress towards the destination? Or if you think of your Lent as a story, has it got the interest and movement you want, or have you lost the plot! It will probably be helpful to look at your feelings quite closely as well as the facts. Do you feel close to God and others on this journey, and encouraged? Or apart, and rather low? How can you offer and receive help?

If you look at the pictures we've used this week, you may be struck by how the first three all show one person being held and helped by another.

Think or talk about the scenes and the feelings of the people shown in them. Then choose one of the pictures and imagine yourself in the story. Put yourself first at a distance, observing; then as the helper; then as the one being helped. What are your feelings? What is God saying to you through them?

Set aside some time to pray for people that you know are hurting in some way, or feeling rejected and isolated. Picture them being held and comforted by God. Listen for anything God may be saying to you about how you can help them as well.

SUNDAY (Third Sunday of Lent)
JERUSALEM, JERUSALEM

Jerusalem is coming into view, and Jesus starts to prepare his disciple band for the crisis and crucifixion that await him there. In terms of this Lenten study, we have one more week before we reach the Passion Narrative, when we will walk the way of the Cross with Christ as best as we can.

We need, then, to be tightening our belt a little, quickening our pace. If some aspects of our plan for Lent have not worked out, now is the time to review them and either try again or try something different. This will make demands on us – but as the saying has it, in Christian discipleship the premiums are all we possess, but the benefits are out of this world.

One further thought: if you have time and can find an appropriate book or video, consider discovering a little about what the Holy Land is like, and especially Jerusalem. I was enormously helped by being able to go there and develop my own picture of the way that Jesus and his disciples were walking.

Almighty God,
whose most dear Son went not up to joy but first he suffered pain,
and entered not into glory before he was crucified:
mercifully grant that we, walking in the way of the cross,
may find it none other than the way of life and peace;
through Jesus Christ your Son our Lord,
who is alive and reigns with you,
in the unity of the Holy Spirit,
one God, now and for ever.

COMMON WORSHIP, Collect for Third Sunday of Lent *

MONDAY
To Jerusalem

Luke 18.31-34

Jesus took the Twelve aside and told them, 'We are going up to Jerusalem, and everything that is written by the prophets about the Son of Man will be fulfilled. He will be handed over to the Gentiles. They will mock him, insult him, spit on him, flog him and kill him. On the third day he will rise again.'

The disciples did not understand any of this. Its meaning was hidden from them, and they did not know what he was talking about.

Imagine you are able to visit Jerusalem, and picture it now as seen on approach, its golden-white stone gleaming in the sun, its walls and towers, and now of course the great golden Dome of the Rock, where once the even more massive and even more gilded Temple of Herod stood. 'Jerusalem the golden ...' – it is an awesome sight.

Every Jew must have carried such a picture in their hearts throughout their lives. There was only one Temple, the place of pilgrimage for vast numbers from all over the world even as Mecca is today. There was only one place of sacrifice, only one Holy of Holies.

We have been steadily losing the spirit of pilgrimage. Tourism and travel per se are not quite the same thing – though in the Holy Land especially tourists often find themselves becoming pilgrims. (This can incidentally be a very appropriate goal for your church if it has visitors.)

The pilgrim is expecting a meeting with the divine, even a transaction, certainly that something will happen. He or she is aware too that it will be a costly affair – in terms of travel, but also of self-offering, for God is not to be collected like a souvenir, but encountered as a sovereign.

All of this must have been clear enough to the disciples. What was not clear to them was the scale of the crisis, the life or death stakes, that lay ahead. They were beginning to glimpse the real nature of Jesus, but

*Jerusalem the
Golden now
– the Dome
of the Rock*

their numbers were probably quite small and there had after all been many other 'maybe-Messiahs' before. And then again, if this really was the One, if the whole crowd, the whole nation, was going to fall in behind him, surely it would be glory, glory all the way?

Not so. It is Jerusalem that stones the prophets, and the prophecies themselves are double-edged.

Our Jerusalem, in this Lenten journey, is both Good Friday and Easter, death and life. So what is our expectation for those feasts this year? The services may be in our diaries – but they are just the scaffolding within which the Spirit can build.

Perhaps this is the time to start to pray for an understanding of what God would have us engage with, explore, experience in the Jerusalem days that lie ahead of us in our journey.

*Jerusalem the golden, Lord,
Magnificent, magnifique,
Moving beyond words.
I too was standing in your courts
O Jerusalem.
I too wondered at the stones I saw.
And all the time you were looking
At the crumbling temple of the Spirit
That is me.
Fill me again, Lord,
And show me your Way.*

TUESDAY
Zacchaeus

Luke 19.1-10

Jesus entered Jericho and was passing through. A man was there by the name of Zacchaeus; he was a chief tax collector and was wealthy. He wanted to see who Jesus was, but being a short man he could not, because of the crowd. So he ran ahead and climbed a sycamore-fig tree to see him, since Jesus was coming that way.

When Jesus reached the spot, he looked up and said to him, 'Zacchaeus, come down immediately. I must stay at your house today.' So he came down at once and welcomed him gladly.

All the people saw this and began to mutter, 'He has gone to be the guest of a 'sinner.''

But Zacchaeus stood up and said to the Lord, 'Look, Lord! Here and now I give half of my possessions to the poor, and if I have cheated anybody out of anything, I will pay back four times the amount.'

Jesus said to him, 'Today salvation has come to this house, because this man, too, is a son of Abraham. For the Son of Man came to seek and to save what was lost.'

The Guinness Book of Records claims that the shortest sermon ever preached – by a curate faced by C H Spurgeon with the request for an impromptu address – went as follows:

'First, Zacchaeus was a man of very small stature; so am I. Second, Zacchaeus was very much up a tree; so am I. Third, Zacchaeus made haste and came down; so will I.'*

I suspect the story of a degree of improvement, and there has been a fashion to approach Bible stories in much the same way, and suggest that they didn't really happen, but were made up later to illustrate a point.

But it is very hard to see how this present episode came to be written up unless it actually happened, and Zacchaeus comes out of it as a most engaging character.

A tax collector in Jericho would have been seriously well off: it was and is a prosperous place, warm and fertile as it nestles in its deep valley by the side of the Jordan, with a history of settlement going back to the dawn of civilisation. If you go there today the locals will gladly point out the tree in question ... but there are many trees to choose from.

Zacchaeus is short for Zechariah, meaning 'a righteous man', and though tax collectors were universally despised, this one was ready to be true to his name. Significantly, he takes the initiative. But equally significantly, Jesus turns the tables on him, seizes that initiative, and completes the conversion.

We could go on to consider how we stereotype people, and fail to see who they are and can be under God because of their job, their size, their fortune. Perhaps we should be being more open, hospitable and generous to those whom we are tempted to write off. Think about it if you need to.

But do think about yourself as well. Have you boxed yourself in too with self-expectations? One way of reading this story is to note that a small break-out on our part can give God the opportunity to break in, and start a virtuous circle of conversion, repentance, blessing, generosity and salvation. And even then he is 'preventing' us in the old sense of going before not to block but to prepare our way. We really can 'begin again' – because of him.

 Prevent us, O Lord, in all our doings with Thy most gracious favour, and further us with Thy continual help; that in all our works, begun, continued, and ended in Thee, we may glorify Thy Holy Name, and finally by Thy mercy obtain everlasting life, through Jesus Christ our Lord.

Book of Common Prayer, Collect at Communion *

WEDNESDAY
Triumphal Entry

Luke 19.28-44
After Jesus had said this, he went on ahead, going up to Jerusalem. As he approached Bethphage and Bethany at the hill called the Mount of Olives, he sent two of his disciples, saying

Ensor, *Christ's Entry in Brussels in 1889*

to them, 'Go to the village ahead of you, and as you enter it, you will find a colt tied there, which no one has ever ridden. Untie it and bring it here. If anyone asks you, "Why are you untying it?" tell him, "The Lord needs it."'

Those who were sent ahead went and found it just as he had told them. As they were untying the colt, its owners asked them, 'Why are you untying the colt?'

They replied, 'The Lord needs it.'

They brought it to Jesus, threw their cloaks on the colt and put Jesus on it. As he went along, people spread their cloaks on the road.

When he came near the place where the road goes down the Mount of Olives, the whole crowd of disciples began joyfully to praise God in loud voices for all the miracles they had seen:

'Blessed is the king who comes in the name of the Lord!'

'Peace in heaven and glory in the highest!'

Some of the Pharisees in the crowd said to Jesus, 'Teacher, rebuke your disciples!'

'I tell you,' he replied, 'if they keep quiet, the stones will cry out.'

As he approached Jerusalem and saw the city, he wept over it and said, 'If you, even you, had only known on this day what would bring you peace – but now it is hidden from your eyes. The days will come upon you when your enemies will build an embankment against you and encircle you and hem you in on every side. They will dash you to the ground, you and the children within your walls. They will not leave one stone on another, because you did not recognize the time of God's coming to you.'

Then he entered the temple area and began driving out those who were selling. 'It is written,' he said to them, "My house will be a house of prayer'; but you have made it 'a den of robbers."

 I only discovered James Ensor's painting recently. It sets the Triumphal Entry in the Brussels Mardi Gras procession of 1889, and caused – as you can imagine – a scandal. Ensor's Christ is partly a self-portrait made at a time when he felt isolated and rejected in the crowd of society around him. He senses a link with the apparently Triumphant Entry.

Jesus plans the event and sets the scene. But once the plan is launched he is out of control. Other people's expectations and agendas are overlaid on his. The drama has begun, and events from now on will have a momentum of their own. 'The very stones will cry out.'

Now this sort of thing happens to us and to the church all the time, and the question is what we are going to make of it. We can lose our voice, as it were, and be co-opted into the story of the world. We can stand aloof as history flows by. We can seek to be Machiavellian manipulators who try to turn events to their own ends. Look at the picture and think where you fit.

Or we can try to find the way of Jesus (where is he in the picture by the way?), a way that is in the world but not of it, in the flow of the story but not subsumed by it. And remember, there are no 'extras' in the cast of life …

 Night is drawing nigh. For all that has been – Thanks!
To all that shall be – Yes!
Dag Hammarskjöld *

THURSDAY
Cleansing the Temple

Luke 19.45-48

Then he entered the temple area and began driving out those who were selling. 'It is written,' he said to them, '"My house will be a house of prayer"; but you have made it 'a den of robbers."'

Every day he was teaching at the temple. But the chief priests, the teachers of the law and the leaders among the people were trying to kill him. Yet they could not find any way to do it, because all the people hung on his words.

Suddenly the Lord you are seeking will come to his temple, prophesied Malachi. Suddenly Jesus is in the Temple precincts and events take a new turn as he takes up the prophet's mantle and confronts the corrupt religious establishment of his time.

This is the inevitable place of crisis. 'Did you not know that I had to be in my Father's house?' are the first words of Jesus in the Gospels. It is Jerusalem that kills the prophets and stones those sent to it, and outside of which no prophet can die.

El Greco,
*Christ Driving
out Traders
from the
Temple*
(detail)

I have sat through more than one sad church council discussion where today's text was wheeled out to oppose having a bookstall in church – when the subject under discussion should have been why there was such a severe discomfort with any action in the name of Christ which would challenge in any way. Since conflict is one of my least favourite ways of spending the day, I can feel some of this from the inside, but when I settle yet again for a safe status quo and good relationships all round, I all too often feel the uncomfortable gaze of Christ in the Temple, facing his destiny.

Societies and structures everywhere will be very happy to commend a 'gentle Jesus, meek and mild' who does not threaten their control. That goes for church structures too. We do not want to engage in struggle for its own sake, nor simple usurp power and gain control for ourselves.

But one look at El Greco's painting is enough to remind us that Jesus was not at all reticent about speaking and acting out God's will when the time was right. Once again there is a 'Jesus way' here – neither avoiding the issues nor becoming bigots about them, but learning to discern the Spirit and speak the word he gives.

It's an awful habit Lord,
I just can't help it.
When I see a pile of papers
I shuffle them straight.
When the family is out of the way
I get the living room back to rights.
And when I walk into church
I simply have to tidy the books,
Line up the chairs,
And sort out the junk by the door.
I suppose it's a helpful sort of a habit,
... some of the time.
I still do it,
But I can hear your voice asking me,
'Am I tidying you up too,
Or really making room for your Spirit to move?
Start, you said,
By cleansing the Temple
Of your heart.

FRIDAY

The Widow's Mite

Luke 21.1-4

As he looked up, Jesus saw the rich putting their gifts into the temple treasury. He also saw a poor widow put in two very small copper coins. 'I tell you the truth,' he said, 'this poor widow has put in more than all the others. All these people gave their gifts out of their wealth; but she out of her poverty put in all she had to live on.'

Doré, *The Widow's Mite*

Jesus is still teaching in the Temple precincts, where Luke convincingly has him throughout this period between the triumphal entry and the Last Supper. I have often tried to imagine the setting – and it has to be said that I am not at all in sympathy with Gustav Doré's nineteenth century Romantic version of it!

A day or so before the present episode there has been absolute mayhem. Presently Jesus is teaching in a highly controversial way. Next he will be speaking of the end times and the Temple's destruction. And Doré has him shining with a heavenly aura, as the action freezes and directs our focus to the suspiciously glamorous widow contributing her mite, as a stage-set book-bound lawyer looks on.

Hmmmph. We are dealing with money here, and however short the passage, the subject is major, and a major issue in the spiritual struggle we all face. Just go back to those church council meetings for a moment ...

Tomorrow the end times: here is an acted parable of the need to be as real as we dare in our actual lives, in dealing with our real money, our real responsibilities and relationships, our real sexuality, the reality of our religion, because in the end there will be no hiding these things. They will be the fabric from which our future is made.

At the heart of this episode, and what makes it such a powerful lesson whether for sorting out church finances or our own lives, is its simple reality. The proportionately outrageously generous gift of the widow surpasses the public patronage of the rich. It is not meant to give them a glow of admiration, but a challenge to a real accounting of their lives.

At the heart of a great deal of spiritual discipline is self-examination in one form or another: a calm assessment of who we are and what we have been up to. It can lead to thanksgiving for the good, and to confession of the bad; to intercession for the grace to be and do better, and to action to share the good we have and be merciful to others.

One of the truths I think we all encounter if we walk this road is that we are capable of a great deal of self-deception. 'Human kind', as T.S Eliot put it, 'cannot bear much reality'. * For that reason we often need the help of another: of the great Other of course, through the Spirit and the Scriptures, and there is no bypassing these; but also of other humans like us, no saints themselves, but able to speak from frailty to frailty and help us to become a little more knowing of ourselves as we are known.

Maybe as the last laps of Lent approach you could consider talking over your journey with another who can share it with you, in whatever tradition and manner is best for you.

Lord, what we know not, teach us; what we have not, give us; what we are not, make us; and all for your name's sake.

Signs of the End

 Luke 21.5-11

Some of his disciples were remarking about how the temple was adorned with beautiful stones and with gifts dedicated to God. But Jesus said, 'As for what you see here, the time will come when not one stone will be left on another; every one of them will be thrown down.'

'Teacher,' they asked, 'when will these things happen? And what will be the sign that they are about to take place?'

He replied: 'Watch out that you are not deceived. For many will come in my name, claiming, 'I am he,' and, 'The time is near.' Do not follow them. When you hear of wars and revolutions, do not be frightened. These things must happen first, but the end will not come right away.'

Then he said to them: 'Nation will rise against nation, and kingdom against kingdom. There will be great earthquakes, famines and pestilences in various places, and fearful events and great signs from heaven.'

The Temple must have made quite an impression on our Galilean visitors. But no sooner have they seen and admired it, than Jesus is speaking of its destruction.

What do you make of the disciples' reaction to Jesus' prophecy? It seems to me almost too calm to be true. I know that for all its grandeur Herod's edifice was widely regarded as not quite proper – but it was still the Temple.

Perhaps, though, you can remember how you yourself or a friend have reacted in the face of a loss. We are often surprisingly calm to start with, and the bewilderment and rage take some time to set in. Sometimes we can stay in that first phase an inappropriately long time, when it is usually labelled as denial.

Jesus is prophesying the end of the world as we know it. Denial would not be a surprising reaction either from the disciples or ourselves. We live most of our lives with a discreet lack of reference to the 100% mortality rate of the human race; and we make our personal and communal plans on the assumption of reasonable continuity and success. It would be strange and probably pathological to do otherwise.

Just occasionally, though, we do need to stand back and look at the whole picture, however hard that is (and the lack of weight given to Jesus' apocalyptic teaching compared with his other words suggests it is pretty hard).

More particularly, I do not think we can properly appreciate what Jesus faced and underwent in Jerusalem without standing back in this way and accepting that for him – and for us if we will follow him – this was a cataclysmic moment, embraced by him because of the cataclysmic consequences for each of us that it involves.

Can I suggest again that there is a Jesus 'middle way' of reacting to this? In this case the other two options are denial on the one hand, and a panicked obsession with the end on the other. The third way is summed up classically as 'to live each day is if it were your last': to get on with living the story of our life, but remember the great narrative in which it is set.

You might like at this point to reflect on your journey so far – not just of Lent but of your life. If you didn't do it earlier, you might find it helpful to draw a pictorial map of it; more scientific types could try a graph; I've even helped people do it with knitting wool! However you tackle it, the idea is to be able to stand back and offer the past, the present and the future to God, open to His will.

Thank you, dear Jesus,
for all that you have given me,
for all that you have taken from me,
for all you have left me.

Thomas More *

Try and find some books or pictures about the Holy Land, or invite someone who has been there to talk about it and show slides. How do you find that the present (with all its politics and problems. commercialisation and religious overlay) and the past (the time of Old and New Testaments, still there in the land and the story) relate to each other?

Re-read Luke 19.28-44, the story of the Triumphal Entry. (It's Wednesday's reading). Then have another look at James Ensor's painting of it, deliberately made not as a re-creation

of the past but a putting of the past into the present. Talk about what you can see in the picture: what links up with what the original day must have been like, and what is different. Remember that Passover in first century Jerusalem was a time of huge crowds, with pilgrim bands arriving from all over the world.

Then picture the scene in your mind, with you on a tower by the gate looking down as Jesus arrives. What are you going to do? What happens next? Do you get to meet Jesus?

Pray for the peace of Jerusalem. You could gather some stones and place them by the candle to symbolise the 'Living Stones' – the Christians of the Holy Land today. You might like to find out more about their needs and concerns. There are many organisations who can help: one is the Jerusalem and Middle East Church Association (www.jmeca.org.uk).

WEEK 5

MOTHERING SUNDAY (Fourth Sunday of Lent)
THE HOUR HAS COME

Mothering Sunday is a sort of half-way stop on the journey of Lent. One of its old names in fact is Refreshment Sunday, and daughters would take simnel cakes to their mothers as the Lenten fast was suspended. (In some places pink hangings were put up in church as well!)

The 'mother' we are remembering is not just mum but Mother Church, and like any break this is a time to enjoy each other's company, swap stories, rebuild our fellowship, before we hit the road again.

A few specially called people apart, we are not asked by God, in fact, to walk this way on our own, nor could we. We are given one another, and we are given the Spirit of Christ among us. We need to take the opportunities we are given to encourage each other and simply have fun together.

Enjoy!

God of compassion,
whose Son Jesus Christ, the child of Mary,
shared the life of a home in Nazareth,
and on the cross drew the whole human family to himself:
strengthen us in our daily living
that in joy and in sorrow
we may know the power of your presence to bind together and to heal;
through Jesus Christ your Son our Lord,
who is alive and reigns with you,
in the unity of the Holy Spirit,
one God, now and for ever.

COMMON WORSHIP, Collect for Mothering Sunday *

WEEK 5 MONDAY
The Tempter Returns

Luke 22.1-6

Now the Feast of Unleavened Bread, called the Passover, was approaching, and the chief priests and the teachers of the law were looking for some way to get rid of Jesus, for they were afraid of the people. Then Satan entered Judas, called Iscariot, one of the Twelve. And Judas went to the chief priests and the officers of the temple guard and discussed with them how he might betray Jesus. They were delighted and agreed to give him money. He consented, and watched for an opportunity to hand Jesus over to them when no crowd was present.

Do you remember that certain way of speaking that we hear repeatedly in the voice-overs of television documentaries. Measured in pace, portentous in construction, it signals authority, and not infrequently doom – especially if the programme concerned is Horizon. This too is the tone of the opening lines of Luke's passion. 'Now drew near the Feast of the Unleavened Bread, the one called the Passover.' In the very first verse of the Gospel itself, Luke had declared his hand: this was, he said, to be the definitive chronicle of what had come to fulfilment in their own days; an orderly account of a new order's birth. Now, as the climax of his account approaches, the crisis of that ultimate regime change is upon us.

As we start on the second half of our journey through Lent, we turn with Jesus towards the Cross. The action slows, the tension heightens, and more than ever we are drawn in from being passers-by to protagonists in a great revolution.

Luke's Gospel is sometimes said to be that for the Gentiles, Matthew's being that for the Jews. This is not really true. Luke's whole frame of reference is thorough-goingly Judaic. It is the Jewish hope that is fulfilled in Jesus – but at a price. Instead of the nations coming to God in Jerusalem, God will go to the nations and Jerusalem – too caught up in its own salvation to offer salvation to the world – will be lost. Luke's first listeners were probably the Jews

Nolde, *The Last Supper* (detail)

and Godfearers of the diaspora – like his dedicatee Theophilus, the friend of God – who were reeling under the news of Jerusalem's utter destruction at the hands of the Romans, still in the lifetime of many who had witnessed the death and resurrection of Christ, when symbolically that destruction was begun as the skies darkened and the curtain of the Temple was torn in two. And the new kingdom founded then is still being built now in our own lives today.

This then is a drama of cosmic proportions, and Luke marks its beginnings by the return of the Satan, who left Jesus after his failed temptation, to return at an opportune time. Now is that time, and now the tempter enters Judas, marginalised in Luke's careful Greek as of the number of the twelve, but not one of them. Judas in Luke's account does not simply offer betrayal, he discusses it and then consents to it. It is his will which is in the balance and which is corrupted.

Lord God Almighty, shaper and ruler of all thy creatures: We pray thee of thy great mercy to guide us to thy will, to make our minds steadfast, to strengthen us against temptation, to put far from us all unrighteousness. Shield us against our foes, seen and unseen; teach us that we may inwardly love thee before all things with a clean mind and a clean body. For thou art our Maker and Redeemer, our help and our comfort, our trust and our hope, now and for evermore.

King Alfred *

TUESDAY
Then Came the Day

Luke 22.7-23

Then came the day of Unleavened Bread on which the Passover lamb had to be sacrificed. Jesus sent Peter and John, saying, 'Go and make preparations for us to eat the Passover.'

'Where do you want us to prepare for it?' they asked.

He replied, 'As you enter the city, a man carrying a jar of water will meet you. Follow him to the house that he enters, and say to the owner of the house, "The Teacher asks: Where is the guest room, where I may eat the Passover with my disciples?" He will show you a large upper room, all furnished. Make preparations there.' They left and found things just as Jesus had told them. So they prepared the Passover.

When the hour came, Jesus and his apostles reclined at the table. And he said to them, 'I have eagerly desired to eat this Passover with you before I suffer. For I tell you, I will not eat it again until it finds fulfilment in the kingdom of God.'

After taking the cup, he gave thanks and said, 'Take this and divide it among you. For I tell you I will not drink again of the fruit of the vine until the kingdom of God comes.' And he took bread, gave thanks and broke it, and gave it to them, saying, 'This is my body given for you; do this in remembrance of me.'

In the same way, after the supper he took the cup, saying, 'This cup is the new covenant in my blood, which is poured out for you. But the hand of him who is going to betray me is with mine on the table. The Son of Man will go as it has been decreed, but woe to that man who betrays him.' They began to question among themselves which of them it might be who would do this.

Judas has made his choice. What will the others choose? Luke singles out Peter and John by name as those sent to make the Passover arrangements for Jesus. What will their choice be? Their track record of understanding is a mixed one. They query Jesus about his plans. Where is the meal to be held? There is perhaps a hint again of disbelief and doubt: finding last-minute accommodation in Jerusalem at Passover was no easy thing. But Jesus is in full command of the situation. As early as chapter 9 Luke had shown him moving purposefully towards Jerusalem, and here he has full fore-knowledge – whether by previous arrangement or spiritual insight – of how matters are to be arranged.

Luke's turn of phrase 'When the hour came' alerts us like the striking of a clock to the coming crisis. Jesus' purpose is the inauguration of the kingdom, and as the disciple band shares what will be its Last Supper with Jesus, he makes explicit the drama that is about to break: ' "I have eagerly desired to eat this Passover with you before I suffer. For I tell you, I will not eat it again until it finds fulfilment in the kingdom of God." After taking the cup, he gave thanks and said, "Take this and divide it among you. For I tell you I will not drink again of the fruit of the vine until the kingdom of God comes." '

Emil Nolde portrayed this moment from the Last Supper in his powerful painting of 1909. Looking back 25 years later on the intense feelings he experienced while working on it he wrote, 'I painted and painted hardly knowing whether it was night or day, whether I was a human being or only a painter. I saw the painting when I went to bed; it confronted me during the night; it faced me when I woke up.' It is a work of astonishing intensity, and we can read reactions of every sort in the faces of the disciples. Will they choose to stay with Christ or not? What will we choose? How do we react in the face of such an intense challenge to make our choice? The kingdom is coming, the world is changing. Where do we stand?

Lord, I want to be there with you and for you
– but I want to hide as well.
Your intensity draws me and frightens me.
Your challenge calls me and daunts me.
I look on your face and see life in all its fullness:
Holiness and horror too.
You look on my face and see …
The self I sought to hide.
Help me to be more truly the me
That you mean me to be:
In the kingdom of our Father.

WEEK 5 WEDNESDAY
Table Talk

Luke 22.24-34

Also a dispute arose among them as to which of them was considered to be greatest. Jesus said to them, 'The kings of the Gentiles lord it over them; and those who exercise authority over them call themselves Benefactors. But you are not to be like that. Instead, the greatest among you should be like the youngest, and the one who rules like the one who serves. For who is greater, the one who is at the table or the one who serves? Is it not the one who is at the table? But I am among you as one who serves. You are those who have stood by me in my trials. And I confer on you a kingdom, just as my Father conferred one on me, so that you may eat and drink at my table in my kingdom and sit on thrones, judging the twelve tribes of Israel.

'Simon, Simon, Satan has asked to sift you as wheat. But I have prayed for you, Simon, that your faith may not fail. And when you have turned back, strengthen your brothers.'

But he replied, 'Lord, I am ready to go with you to prison and to death.'

Jesus answered, 'I tell you, Peter, before the rooster crows today, you will deny three times that you know me.'

This whole section of table-talk is as it stands unique to Luke, though the dispute over primacy recurs elsewhere. It is set at the centre of this carefully balanced first part of the passion narrative, with Satan's challenge to sift Simon Peter at its own centre.

Luke uses the themes with which we are familiar from the Lord's Prayer to explore the coming of the kingdom and its challenge as to whose will is to be done. As the disciples share the bread together that is to be the bread of the kingdom day (an equally valid translation of 'daily bread'), the issue of their temptation, and particularly Peter's, comes to the fore, and his need for deliverance from evil.

Satan's work can already be seen, as Luke lays out the matter, in the dispute between the disciples. If the kingdom is not going to come in purely Judaic terms because the Jewish state is too concerned with its own power and survival, it will hardly do for the new kingdom to simply replicate the equally self-concerned lordship of the Gentiles. No: doing good, being a benefactor, is not about getting a name for yourself or your name on things, but is necessarily a matter seeking the good of others even at cost to oneself. As Jesus models it. To receive the kingdom is also to receive such a self-denying ordinance in matters of kingship. It is a lesson that the disciples were slow to learn then and disciples are slow to learn now.

Luke, though, does not at all present this as a reason to lose hope. Writing from within the Judaic tradition of the book of Job, he sees the Satan's power as thoroughly circumscribed vis-à-vis the sovereignty of God. The Satan has to ask to tempt the disciples; he asks to sift Simon Peter – but the word 'sift' implies that the good seed will survive to bear fruit; the effect of his testing is subject to the power of Christ's prayer, and Peter will indeed go on to strengthen his brothers. Jesus, as throughout Luke's Passion, is fully aware of the whole picture, and has so to speak already factored in the faltering faith of the disciples, and seen beyond it to victory. They will go through their charade with the swords, he sees it all, and as it is written so it will be fulfilled.

Here I am Lord,
Send me!
I will go Lord, where you ...
Where?
Oh.
I hadn't thought that ...
I hadn't really thought.
It's a good job
You're praying for me,
Good Lord.

THURSDAY
Gethsemane

Luke 22.35-46

Then Jesus asked them, 'When I sent you without purse, bag or sandals, did you lack anything?'

'Nothing,' they answered.

He said to them, 'But now if you have a purse, take it, and also a bag; and if you don't have a sword, sell your cloak and buy one. It is written: 'And he was numbered with the transgressors' ; and I tell you that this must be fulfilled in me. Yes, what is written about me is reaching its fulfilment.' The disciples said, 'See, Lord, here are two swords.' 'That is enough,' he replied.

Gethsemane
Chapel,
Coventry
Cathedral

Jesus went out as usual to the Mount of Olives, and his disciples followed him. On reaching the place, he said to them, 'Pray that you will not fall into temptation.' He withdrew about a stone's throw beyond them, knelt down and prayed, 'Father, if you are willing, take this cup from me; yet not my will, but yours be done.' An angel from heaven appeared to him and strengthened him. And being in anguish, he prayed more earnestly, and his sweat was like drops of blood falling to the ground. When he rose from prayer and went back to the disciples, he found them asleep, exhausted from sorrow. 'Why are you sleeping?' he asked them. 'Get up and pray so that you will not fall into temptation.'

Now the enemy must be faced. The swords are a diversion: the real action will be spiritual. Jesus must himself model the defeat of the tempter, and it is here in Gethsemane that he has his real agony, not on the Cross, where the victory will no longer be in doubt.

Matthew and Mark focus on the disciples' lack of commitment to prayer in the garden: Luke's attention is all on Jesus, and it is he who adds the details of the bloody sweat and the strengthening angel – even strangely the detail of kneeling, which was not the usual Jewish posture for prayer: another sign perhaps of Luke taking the new kingdom outside the boundaries of the old. His wording too firms up the focus on obedience to God's will: and the temptation for him as for the disciples is to step outside it.

Luke gives us a careful balance between agony and assistance, testing and victory. Jesus suffers dreadfully. He shows us that suffering, wrestling with God's will, going through spiritual battle, is not a sign of desertion – either by us or God. But Jesus is also helped wonderfully by an angel – depicted memorably for me in a mosaic in the Gethsemane Chapel of Coventry Cathedral, which glows with gold, but is seen through a crown of wrought iron thorns. The cup the angel holds is simultaneously the cup of Christ's suffering and the chalice of the eucharist.

There is a lesson here for us as we are confronted by our own powerlessness in the face of public crises and private catastrophes. We are reminded of the power of God, against which even evil must break. We are shown the prayer of Christ, effective for him and for us. And we are offered the possibility of ministry, even when like Peter we seem to fail the test.

I'll be there, Lord;
Thank you so much for the invitation.
See you on the day ...
Oh no, I've done it again.
Let my enthusiasm, my desire to please
Run way ahead of what I can really handle.
When the day comes, Lord,
It's a good thing you'll be there with me.
Without you I couldn't face it.
With you, we might just get through.

FRIDAY

The Heart of Darkness

Luke 22.47-53

While he was still speaking a crowd came up, and the man who was called Judas, one of the Twelve, was leading them. He approached Jesus to kiss him, but Jesus asked him, 'Judas, are you betraying the Son of Man with a kiss?' When Jesus' followers saw what was going to happen, they said, 'Lord, should we strike with our swords?' And one of them struck the servant of the high priest, cutting off his right ear. But Jesus answered, 'No more of this!' And he touched the man's ear and healed him. Then Jesus said to the chief priests, the officers of the temple guard, and the elders, who had come for him, 'Am I leading a rebellion, that you have come with swords and clubs? Every day I was with you in the temple courts, and you did not lay a hand on me. But this is your hour – when darkness reigns.'

Luke's conversational excursus has slowed the action, built the passing of time into the drama; but now events once again march forward, and while Jesus is still speaking the crowd burst in.

Judas' intention is to use his disciple's greeting of his Rabbi with a kiss to show the guards which of the figures in the darkness is the Rabbi Jesus. In Luke's Gospel he is intercepted by Jesus before he can make the kiss. His intention is fore-known, and his action gently but decisively rebuked.

When the disciples go on to ask whether they should strike with their swords, their question is framed in a way that expects the answer yes, and they do not even wait for the answer. But once again the disciples are floundering on the edge of the action. Jesus does not seem to expect otherwise. Instead he quietly calms them down and heals the severed ear. We are a long way from the in-your-face brutal realism of Mel Gibson's film of the Passion. The inner peace of Christ as he approaches the Cross spills out in Luke's Passion as a sign of hope to those who believe in him, and of contradiction to those who cannot comprehend His Way.

Contrast Gibson's portrayal of the arrest, true perhaps to the reality of our inhumanity, with that by Giotto in the remarkable fresco cycle in the Scrovegni Chapel at Padua, which is true to the heavenly power play behind the earthly events. All the human action is there in a swirl of spears and slashes, but every gaze leads us to the still centre of the painting, Christ's face, unmoved by Judas' attempt to engulf him with a kiss – obscuring (but failing to obscure) Christ in a way that was totally daring in terms of the artistic conventions of the day.

After the arrest, Luke's Jesus does not wait for his captors to question him. He initiates the conversation with a speech that turns the tables on them, showing the powerlessness in their apparent power, not just in this brief encounter but in the narrative as a whole. This is their hour, the hour when darkness seems to reign; but its victory is illusion, and will soon be exposed as the sham it is.

Lighten our darkness, we beseech Thee, O Lord, and by Thy great mercy, defend us from all perils and dangers of this night, for the sake of Thy Son, Jesus Christ our Lord.

BOOK OF COMMON PRAYER, Third Collect at Evening Prayer *

Giotto,
*The Kiss
of Judas*

SATURDAY
The Look of Christ's Love

Luke 22.54-62

Then seizing him, they led him away and took him into the house of the high priest. Peter followed at a distance. But when they had kindled a fire in the middle of the courtyard and had sat down together, Peter sat down with them. A servant girl saw him seated there in the firelight. She looked closely at him and said, 'This man was with him.'

But he denied it. 'Woman, I don't know him,' he said.

A little later someone else saw him and said, 'You also are one of them.'

'Man, I am not!' Peter replied.

About an hour later another asserted, 'Certainly this fellow was with him, for he is a Galilean.'

Peter replied, 'Man, I don't know what you're talking about!' Just as he was speaking, the rooster crowed. The Lord turned and looked straight at Peter. Then Peter remembered the word the Lord had spoken to him: 'Before the rooster crows today, you will disown me three times.' And he went outside and wept bitterly.

Peter in the courtyard goes on to deny Christ as predicted, one betrayal mirroring another. His language is sharp and colloquial, but Luke stops him short of calling down a curse on himself as he does in Mark, and while the passage has colour, it is not laboured, and Peter's tears at the end are observed but not unexpected. Even at this point our eyes are being drawn to Jesus, who is placed in the courtyard by Luke, himself to observe the betrayal, judge it, and be unshaken by it.

And now we have to face a problem with this impassive passion of Luke's; a problem likely to be felt anyway by our current generation. It comes in two parts. First, how human is this Jesus? We read his action here more in terms of a comic hero than a tragicomic correlate of ourselves. We like heroes in our cartoons and computer games, but are not comfortable with them in reality. And if he is not fully human, how does that help us who are? Secondly, and related to it, how real is this victory? Disenchanted by the stage-managed reportage of recent wars and the constant spinning of the news, we are disturbed by and disbelieving of a story that has so settled an outcome. Cut to Judas, suing the early church for libel; read on for analysis from our Middle Eastern correspondent who has been speaking to the centurion.

But I think the real challenge may lie a level deeper. There is a scandal of particularity at play. Are we willing to allow that ever, in a certain place, at a certain place, in a certain life, God can act and indeed has acted decisively? And that as a result all that we are and all the flux that we inhabit is relativised by it? We are used to being the critic, the observer, the independent arbitrator of our own times. The echo of newspaper titles is deliberate! But only by allowing another – the one whose critique is always selfless – to be the critic of all of us can we escape the endlessly reflecting mirrors of a world made up of mutually competing criticism, continually competing selves.

To put it another way, we have to ask ourselves at this point of the passion, are we content not just to look on Christ, whether in admiration, anguish, disbelief or disgust – but to let him look on us. Now that's scary. As the doggerel poem puts it: 'I think I'd sooner frizzle up, i' the flames of a burning 'ell, Than stand and look into 'is face, And 'ear 'is voice say "Well …".' More seriously, it is a look which is full of love but which demands we accept accountability for our own lives – be we Judas, Peter or David.

I've been collecting pictures, Lord,
Pictures of you.
Pictures I like
And ones I don't.
I've become a bit of a critic:
Help!
Help me to remember that
You're the one
Who does the judging
At the end of this exhibition.

We've been using the metaphor of a meal for these study sessions – a starter, a main course and a pudding. This week, how about sharing some real food as well! Treat yourself if you're on your own; or all bring something tasty to share if you're in a group. What food do you enjoy the most? Do you like to eat alone, or in company? How much does it matter to you to eat with your family and friends?

 Have another look at Luke 22.7-23, the account of the Last Supper. (It's Tuesday's passage.) Different artists have painted the scene in very different ways. Most of us know Leonardo da Vinci's version with the disciples lined up along one side of a table. Watch out too for Tintoretto's  painting in the Prado which shows one disciple debagging another to have his feet washed, and Duccio's which has Peter scratching his head in bafflement. Nolde focuses by contrast on the emotions that are present and the central wonder of the first eucharist. Imagine yourself in the scene – perhaps as a servant waiting on. What do you see? Does Christ have anything to say to you?

You could end your meal by sharing wine and bread, with a prayer of thanks for all God's gifts – an agape or a eucharist as your church tradition allows. It is a sign that Jesus is with you as you journey towards Easter together.

PASSION SUNDAY (Fifth Sunday of Lent)
BEHOLD THE MAN

If you flip ahead a few pages you'll see that the images we'll be sharing are very powerful indeed. On this Passion Sunday our focus starts to narrow down onto the Passion of the Cross, and onto the suffering of Christ.

Passion and passivity are closely related: they are both about having things done to us. And however much Luke's Christ is in control of his destiny, there is a marked change at this point in the gospel as Jesus is handed over. Now he will do much less and be content to be done to.

This is something with which nearly all of us can identify. Youthful vigour gives way to the aches of middle age and the incapacity of advanced years. Great plans become embroiled in even greater frustrations. The woes of the world bear in on us.

Today could be a good time to pray for all those who are sharing the Passion of Christ in their powerlessness and pain, for individuals we know, for the masses we do not know, and for whole societies who struggle to break free into God's future for them. Picture those you are praying for by the Cross, but then invite the Risen Lord into the scene.

Most merciful God,
who by the death and resurrection of your Son Jesus Christ
delivered and saved the world:
grant that by faith in him who suffered on the cross
we may triumph in the power of his victory;
through Jesus Christ your Son our Lord,
who is alive and reigns with you,
in the unity of the Holy Spirit,
one God, now and for ever.
COMMON WORSHIP, Collect for Fifth Sunday of Lent *

WEEK 6 · MONDAY

The Man of Sorrows

Luke 22.63-71

The men who were guarding Jesus began mocking and beating him. They blindfolded him and demanded, 'Prophesy! Who hit you?' And they said many other insulting things to him.

At daybreak the council of the elders of the people, both the chief priests and teachers of the law, met together, and Jesus was led before them. 'If you are the Christ,' they said, 'tell us.'

Jesus answered, 'If I tell you, you will not believe me, and if I asked you, you would not answer. But from now on, the Son of Man will be seated at the right hand of the mighty God.'

They all asked, 'Are you then the Son of God?'

He replied, 'You are right in saying I am.'

Then they said, 'Why do we need any more testimony? We have heard it from his own lips.'

We have reached an important interlude in the Passion according to Luke. I have been describing how in Luke's narrative Jesus is very much the hero, the victor-elect, the still centre as the catastrophe unfolds around him.

But in brute reality he has been arrested, held in custody by ungentle soldiers, and is about to be put on trial for his life and face a tortured death. It will not be Luke's way to dwell on these things, but here – for a moment – he reminds us how it must have been. The note of mockery is Luke's own, and it is perhaps typical of him that the psychological distress is set alongside the physical; typical too that the unwritten sub-text is always that the mockers are mocked by their own ignorance, just as the judges are to be judged. The basic point is made though, that here is a man, and here is man's inhumanity to man: the man of sorrows, acquainted with grief.

Umbrian
Master,
*The Man of
Sorrows*

Ever since the National Gallery bought the little 13th century panel by an unknown Umbrian artist and re-united it with its sister piece of the Virgin and Child, I have been unable to imagine Christ as the Man of Sorrows without remembering its ghastly, even ghoulish, image of a green-fleshed cadaver-like Christ. I wonder how you react to it? It was painted very much under the influence of St Francis and sets out deliberately to evoke a reaction, to ask us to give our verdict, and perhaps give our lives.

Luke goes into very little detail of the trial of the Christ. He comes straight to the point of direct question – 'Are you the Christ? Are you the Son of God?' What matters is who this man is. What matters too is our own verdict on that. Jesus simply reflects back our answers to us: literally, 'You say that I am.' But into that Luke inserts Jesus' judgement on the justice he is facing. If he answers himself, they will not believe him; and if he asks them to answer, they will not. The court is rigged. Its outcome of the court is as certain in human terms as the outcomes of all such courts are.

The irony, of course, is that in heavenly terms the outcome of this process is also certain, and quite the opposite of appearances.

So, Lord, you want me to come to you
Just as I am
As the old hymn puts it.
I'm not too used to doing that.
And perhaps I'm not too sure either
About you, just as you are.
Perhaps we could start
By exchanging a few e-mails,
And then a bite to eat
Somewhere nice –
Just to see how it goes.
And then …
And then it may be too late.

WEEK 6

TUESDAY
Dignity and Disability

Luke 22.63-64

The men who were guarding Jesus began mocking and beating him. They blindfolded him and demanded, 'Prophesy! Who hit you?' And they said many other insulting things to him.

We need to stay with the mocking and beating a little longer. Unlike Luke, we cannot pass over it so easily.

Two things are colliding here that can leave us feeling very uncomfortable. On the one hand there is the gruesome reality of suffering and disability. On the other there is the hidden truth that this corpse-like figure is the Christ, the Saviour of the World, the only human in whom we can find true life and power.

As a society we engage with the rhetoric of dignity in disablement; but we do in fact find it acutely difficult, I think, to see real people with disabilities as dignitaries – be it in their poverty, ill health, physical impairment or difficulty in learning. I am certainly still only at the beginning of this journey myself. I owe a debt of thanks to hospitals where I have worked and visited and where I have encountered men and women with multiple paralysis, with profoundly delayed development, in their bravery, their bolshiness, their sexuality and their death. And I will always remember Derek, the crucifer in a church I served, whose lurching along the nave broke through our boundaries, and Kenny whose manipulative loving tested them, and Jane who gathered these people and many others under her wings and demanded that we be church with them.

But can we go so far as to see worth not only in the suffering person but in suffering itself and the cross as making it worthy, as some have done? No, that is probably to go too far, though I remain challenged. Not only does the idea tempt us to too easy a glossing over of real people's real hurt, but it is too easily co-opted by the forces of domination. But we can and must say that even as in Christ all is made life, so his life is found in the vale of suffering too. If humankind has dignity, it has dignity in its suffering. If we deny that, we begin to deny our own humanity.

Perhaps the call to us, then, from this victimised victor is to come before one another and before God truly as we are, in our ability and our disability, if we are to truly find life in him.

Thanks be to Thee, my Lord Jesus Christ,
For all the benefits
Which Thou hast won for me;
For all the pains and insults
Which Thou hast borne for me.
O Most Merciful Redeemer,
Friend and Brother;
May I know Thee more clearly,
Love Thee more dearly,
And follow Thee more nearly,
Day by day.
St Richard of Chichester *

WEDNESDAY
Man of Righteousness

Bosch,
*Christ
Mocked*

Luke 23.1-5

Then the whole assembly rose and led him off to Pilate. And they began to accuse him, saying, 'We have found this man subverting our nation. He opposes payment of taxes to Caesar and claims to be Christ, a king.'

So Pilate asked Jesus, 'Are you the king of the Jews?'

'Yes, it is as you say,' Jesus replied.

Then Pilate announced to the chief priests and the crowd, 'I find no basis for a charge against this man.'

But they insisted, 'He stirs up the people all over Judea by his teaching. He started in Galilee and has come all the way here.'

If only all justice was so quick! 'Are you the king of the Jews?' asks Pilate. 'As you say,' says Jesus. 'Charge dismissed,' says Pilate.

True, the other gospel writers do not even bother to have the Jews state their charge to Pilate as Luke takes care to do. 'We have found this man subverting our nation. He opposes payment of taxes to Caesar and claims to be Christ, a King.' But what Luke is trying to do here is drive home a point that was perhaps crucial to the offer of the gospel in the Roman-controlled world of the Jewish diaspora. The Jewish authorities brought Jesus before Pilate on a necessarily Roman and political charge, rather than a Jewish and theological one. And Pilate unsurprisingly threw it out immediately as a fiction. Jesus was as innocent in Roman terms as he was righteous, so Luke asserts, in Judaic ones.

The Jewish leaders now, and Pilate later, do not come out of this well. Considering the Sanhedrin's distaste for Roman rule, their presentation of Christ as a subversive is ingenuous to say the least. Jesus again simply reflects back his questioners' words to them. 'That's what you are saying.' His calm forms a mirror in which others are seen for who they are – in which we are seen for who we are.

One of the real joys, Lord,
Of a minor dignitary's life
Is a good thick cushion
On my stall in church.
In my position
I reckon I deserve a bit of comfort
– As I sit in today's Sanhedrin
Passing judgment on the world.

Before Herod

Luke 23.6-12

On hearing this, Pilate asked if the man was a Galilean. When he learned that Jesus was under Herod's jurisdiction, he sent him to Herod, who was also in Jerusalem at that time.

When Herod saw Jesus, he was greatly pleased, because for a long time he had been wanting to see him. From what he had heard about him, he hoped to see him perform some miracle. He plied him with many questions, but Jesus gave him no answer. The chief priests and the teachers of the law were standing there, vehemently accusing him. Then Herod and his soldiers ridiculed and mocked him. Dressing him in an elegant robe, they sent him back to Pilate. That day Herod and Pilate became friends – before this they had been enemies.

At this point Luke includes an excursus. Throughout his Gospel we see him drawing on a special source of information about Herod – perhaps from Joanna the wife of Chuza, the manager of Herod's household. Whatever its source, what follows in verses 5 to 12 is a privileged account of Jesus half tried half shown off before Herod at Pilate's behest.

What are we to make of this pantomime? Jesus is silent throughout and I am minded to heed his example. There is something of a tradition, from the mediaeval mystery plays through to the Herod-as-Elvis of Jesus Christ Superstar of turning the mockery back on Herod and the Jewish leaders. In terms of drama it gives a satisfying revenge and comic relief at the same time. But in terms of human history it only encourages the inhumanity that is taking Christ to the cross. Funny horned headdresses for the high priests today: stars sown onto their jackets tomorrow. Silence seems a better alternative.

Perhaps that is why I am so disturbed by the painting of *Christ Mocked* by that most disturbing of artists, Hieronymus Bosch. The figures crowd in on Christ and on us. Their expressions show a cynical and brutal amusement, and they are caricatured and dehumanised in their dress – note the animal collar on the top right hand soldier reminding us of the besetting beasts of the Psalm 22, the Islamic crescent and Jewish star on the headdress of the man lower left, the strange

crossbow bolt in the hat of the man above him. Perhaps it isn't so easy after all to escape the compromises and ambiguities of society.

Luke tries to reinforce the claim of secular innocence for Christ and political acceptability for his Church. How comfortable are we, I wonder, with this as well? The Church of England, my own denomination, has traded for a long time on its political acceptability, thankfully not always to the total loss of a critical edge towards the politics of its day. As affairs seem to drift towards disestablishment and an American or French style separation between religion and state, will we in the C of E find that we are left without clothes to wear in public life, or at least only fancy dress? With what would we clothe ourselves, if we were to start again? What would we wish to say to the society in which we live, as we stand together at the bar of God's justice? Or would we decide just to stand aloof?

Jesus' enigmatic smile leaves us wondering: but though he was no political Messiah, his whole incarnation was in the end a political act, a claiming of the kingship for God. Where are we being called to incarnate God's kingdom now?

Go forth into the world in peace; Be of good courage:
Hold fast that which is good; Render to no man evil for evil;
Strengthen the faint-hearted; Support the weak; Help the afflicted;
Honour all men; Love and serve the Lord;
Rejoice in the Power of the Holy Spirit.

A Valediction *

WEEK 6 FRIDAY
The Weakness of Pilate

Luke 23.13-22

Pilate called together the chief priests, the rulers and the people, and said to them, 'You brought me this man as one who was inciting the people to rebellion. I have examined him in your presence and have found no basis for your charges against him. Neither has Herod, for he sent him back to us; as you can see, he has done nothing to deserve death. Therefore, I will punish him and then release him.'

With one voice they cried out, 'Away with this man! Release Barabbas to us!' (Barabbas had been thrown into prison for an insurrection in the city, and for murder.) Wanting to release Jesus, Pilate appealed to them again. But they kept shouting, 'Crucify him! Crucify him!'

For the third time he spoke to them: 'Why? What crime has this man committed? I have found in him no grounds for the death penalty. Therefore I will have him punished and then release him.'

Jesus is brought back from Herod to Pilate. Luke as we have seen is concerned to establish that Jesus is innocent of all charges, and indeed that Pilate fully recognises this and makes strenuous efforts to have him released. Symbolically, Luke has Pilate make three attempts so to do.

Why, we may well wonder, was it such a struggle? If the matter was in Pilate's hands, why did he not simply release the prisoner and be done with it?

The constitutive answer to that question is a matter of historical fact rather than interpretation: for right or wrong that is how it happened. But by making so much of Pilate's belief in Jesus' innocence, Luke inevitably sets him up in this narrative for a monumental display of judicial weakness and pragmatism. Just as the Jewish authorities have themselves had Jesus arrested and seek his death out of fear for the people (22.2) so Pilate is intimidated by the crowd and fearful of how things could be made to look if he let Jesus go (or so John tells us in his chapter 19).

We come back to the matter of corrupted wills. Pilate's own mind is too easily swayed. He surrenders responsibility and surrenders Jesus to the will of his accusers. Behind the scenes, God's will will indeed be done; or better, will not be thwarted whatever we do: but this is at the cost of Jesus' life, for while there is nothing that cannot be redeemed, even death, there is also no preventing the immediate consequences and costs of our actions.

Sarcophagus of Domitilla, Christ before Pilate (detail)

Pilate stands in the tradition as a rather pathetic reminder of how easy and how disastrous it is to wash our hands of responsibility. Luke does not include the action which only Matthew records and which has passed into our language as a synonym for such evasion, but we need to pause at the point where Pilate's hands are as it were still wet from the washing, and ask ourselves how it is with us and our facing of responsibilities today.

I do not see this challenge as a cause or justification for rushing to take sides on every issue and confront every falling short in the society around us. I am minded more to remember the bracelet one of my children wears which has on it the motto W W J D: What Would Jesus Do? If that sounds too cross-cultural for you, remember instead how many times you have prayed, 'Your will be done.' As always in matters of faith, we come back to the person of Christ: his teaching, his example, his character. What is his will for us, here, now?

*God grant me the
SERENITY to accept the things I cannot change,
COURAGE to change the things I can, and
WISDOM to know the difference.*

Reinhold Niebuhr *

WEEK 6 SATURDAY
Handed Over

Luke 23.23-25

But with loud shouts they insistently demanded that he be crucified, and their shouts prevailed. So Pilate decided to grant their demand. He released the man who had been thrown into prison for insurrection and murder, the one they asked for, and surrendered Jesus to their will.

One of the earliest artistic attempts to depict the hand-washing is on a panel from the Sarcophagus of Domitilla of fourth century Rome. Pilate on the far right turns away from the action, cornered, perplexed and defeated. Just to the left of the hand-washing scene stands Christ, more prince than prisoner, larger than life and leading the way. The iconography could not be more clear.

Of course, it is simplistic to imagine that there is any way that we can fully determine the answer to that question 'What would Jesus do?', whether in respect of some of the major ethical issues we face

or some of the very practical and personal choices that we have to make. But it is still the right question, because it asks us to not just to find something to say in a particular case, but to seek to live in the image of Christ in all we are and do. The fact that specific answers are so difficult to construct becomes then a timely reminder that Jesus also warned us not to act as judges over our fellow human beings, however much we think we see them contradicting his way.

So the challenge remains: in the crises which surround you today – what are you doing, and what would Jesus do; and to the extent that those differ, what is to be done about it? We must never underestimate the importance of small-scale, personal response even in the face of huge and impersonal problems. We are standing, remember, at the foot of just one man's cross, remembering just one brief life, and yet they changed the world. The surrender of Jesus, his handing over, before which he is quite passive, which stands at the heart of the way to the Cross in Luke, is not the end but the beginning.

These old carvings, Lord:
They seem to come to us from another world.
A world in which our faith
Became suddenly respectable,
Part of the power-play.
But the more I read the papers
The less I understand
About our world now.
And the Christian faith
Is back on trial for its life.
Help me, Lord,
To let my weakness
Become a strength for you.

Coming to terms with our own power and our own powerlessness is part of the spiritual journey. As the opener for this week's study, take some time to reflect on your own experience of these two things. More generally, what situations leave you feeling helpless, 'done to', or 'out of it' – and what form does that feeling take for you?

Read Luke 22.63-23.3 again (the readings for Monday to Wednesday).

Now look at Bosch's painting of *Christ Mocked*. I think it is perhaps the most disturbing image that I have used in this book. What do you make of the expressions of the people in it – both the tormentors and Christ? He seems strangely detached – almost smiling. They smile too, but the evil is palpable. The action is frozen, and the violence under the surface, but it is all the more worrying for that.

What has this got to say to us about the so very familiar account of the Passion? What has it got to say about the institutionalized violence of our society, and the dark side of even our good endeavours that we would rather ignore?

 Our prayer this week is for the suffering, and particularly for those who suffer behind closed doors – either simply through reserve, or because others do not really want to listen, or because they are in the grip of the torturer or the terrorist, the bully or the corrupted bureaucrat, and there seems no way out.

WEEK 7

PALM SUNDAY (Holy Week, Sixth Sunday of Lent)
THE VICTORY OF THE CROSS

At the heart of Palm Sunday and Holy Week is the simple reading and hearing, enacting and watching of the story of Christ's passion. Just as at Christmas we seek to go to the manger in heart and mind to share in the joy, now we are impelled to walk too in the way of the cross.

We are back to the beginning of our Lenten theme: back to history as his story and his story as our story. Of course we know how the story ends, the great triumph, but we are required both in Holy Week and in our lives never to be triumphalist, but always to walk the way of Jesus with tender feet and tender love.

Whatever else you do this coming Holy Week, stay with the story.

Almighty and everlasting God,
who in your tender love towards the human race sent your Son our Saviour
Jesus Christ
to take upon him our flesh
and to suffer death upon the cross:
grant that we may follow the example of his patience and humility,
and also be made partakers of his resurrection;
through Jesus Christ your Son our Lord,
who is alive and reigns with you,
in the unity of the Holy Spirit,
one God, now and for ever.

Common Worship, Collect for Palm Sunday *

MONDAY in Holy Week
A Very Public Passion

Luke 23.26-31

As they led him away, they seized Simon from Cyrene, who was on his way in from the country, and put the cross on him and made him carry it behind Jesus. A large number of people followed him, including women who mourned and wailed for him. Jesus turned and said to them, 'Daughters of Jerusalem, do not weep for me; weep for yourselves and for your children. For the time will come when you will say, "Blessed are the barren women, the wombs that never bore and the breasts that never nursed!" Then

"they will say to the mountains, 'Fall on us!'
and to the hills, 'Cover us!' "

For if men do these things when the tree is green, what will happen when it is dry?'

'They led him away.' Led like a lamb to the slaughter, we remember. We pick up the story in chapter 23 verse 26. For Jesus now it is a matter of passion, of passivity; of suffering, of suffering others to do with him what they would. Simon of Cyrene in Libya, up in Jerusalem for the Passover visit of a lifetime, is co-opted into the passion, suffering with the Christ in whom it seems he came to believe, since Mark

Bassano, *The Way to Calvary*

calls him the father of Alexander and Rufus as if these were well known to his readers.*

It is all very public, as the gruesome procession winds its way through the suqs and streets of Jerusalem to the Place of the Skull.

Luke, storyteller that he is, makes the most of the scene – a gift to the Mel Gibsons of this world. A large crowd, he tells us, follows on, amongst whom – a typically Lukan touch that we must come back to – are women, wailing and mourning, who historians tell us would have offered opiates to the prisoner. Bassano's painting captures for me something of the crowded drama of the scene – even if his focus is on Veronica and her cloth, which is less scriptural!

Jesus, though, is in no mood to seek oblivion. Instead he confronts Jerusalem with its real cause for wailing. A catastrophe is round the corner, long predicted by the prophets but now as a matter of historical record about to come true. Jerusalem, within the lifetime of many of those there would be razed to the ground by the Romans.

Any crucifixion was designedly a public spectacle; but this one was public too because it concerned a public matter, a national crisis. Jesus offers a rabbinic-style comment to the crowd: 'If men do these things when the tree is green, what will happen when it is dry?' To paraphrase: if this is what happens to a just man, what will happen to the unjust? If this is what happens when the plant is still growing, what sort of destruction will come upon it when it is dead?

Jesus comments on the crisis as a Jew to Jews, in a Jewish way. Luke has been making it clear throughout his Gospel that God is acting in a new way to redeem his people, but that his people – in their corporate and official capacity – are finding this extremely difficult to accept. Many of them would have agreed with the premise – that the Messiah was still awaited. But that this was the one? Putative Messiahs from the aristocracy were plausible; lesser figures who led rebellions could be accommodated; those who withdrew into the wilderness could be marginalised; but this thorn in the flesh who simply started to behave as if the kingdom was coming and bypassed their whole system ...?

I carried a cross once – one Good Friday:
a cross without splinters, a cross without nails.
The crowd were polite, and ignored me.
I'd probably have done the same
in Jerusalem.

Before the Cross

Chagall, *White Crucifixion*

We tend to come before the Cross thinking of Jesus dying that our sins, mine and yours, individually, might be forgiven. And that is true. But 'you' in the New Testament tends to be in the plural, not the singular; and the main thrust of Jesus' proclamation is the kingdom of God, a way of being together under God's rule that is open to all who will receive it. By taking its rule from a just and loving God who gives us radical freedom, this kingdom uniquely saves us from the injustice, malice and domination of our human systems of power.

Seen this way, the Jewish authorities were perhaps right to see in Jesus a fundamental threat to society as they knew it, in which the Law and the Temple stood proxy for God's rule, and claimed to fill the space for him. Who was it who could dare to supplant them and re-define, even re-occupy that space, without blasphemy?

Before we pass on, look for a moment at Chagall's *White Crucifixion* and see how still in our own day the future of the Jewish people and Jewish state is at issue. Chagall places Christ back into the context of his Jewish heritage, images of which replace the traditional instruments of the Passion of earlier devotional art. His loincloth is a prayer shawl. Around him victims of pogroms flee for their lives. Is Christ dying with them, for them, or even against them? This public Passion poses a public question: who is this man? And what does it all mean?

What is the future of our state, and of our identity as the people of God? Do they depend on this man on a cross? Pause for a moment, and consider your verdict …

How is it Lord,
That you were born a Jew,
But of all peoples
The Jews have been the most marginalised?
You are one with them,
You came to save them,
And now
You persecute them
Or so we make it.
If only, Lord …
Perhaps, Lord …
Could it be so?
Lord?

WEEK 7

WEDNESDAY in Holy Week
A Pointed Question

Luke 23.32-43

Two other men, both criminals, were also led out with him to be executed. When they came to the place called the Skull, there they crucified him, along with the criminals – one on his right, the other on his left. Jesus said, 'Father, forgive them, for they do not know what they are doing.' And they divided up his clothes by casting lots.

The people stood watching, and the rulers even sneered at him. They said, 'He saved others; let him save himself if he is the Christ of God, the Chosen One. The soldiers also came up and mocked him. They offered him wine vinegar and said, 'If you are the king of the Jews, save yourself.'

There was a written notice above him, which read: THIS IS THE KING OF THE JEWS.

One of the criminals who hung there hurled insults at him: 'Aren't you the Christ? Save yourself and us!' But the other criminal rebuked him. 'Don't you fear God,' he said, 'since you are under the same sentence? We are punished justly, for we are getting what our deeds deserve. But this man has done nothing wrong.' Then he said, 'Jesus, remember me when you come into your kingdom.' Jesus answered him, 'I tell you the truth, today you will be with me in paradise.'

The narrative moves us on to Golgotha, the place of crucifixion. Luke does not dwell as others do on the brute facts of the execution. They were well enough known to exonerate him from any charge of glossing over. The idea that the suffering was itself a focus of piety rather than what we might call a necessary evil lay long in the future. Without the need either to shock his hearers into remembrance or draw them into devotion, Luke is free to focus on what matters to him the most: Christ's refusal to give evil for evil, so that even in his torturous death he lives the new life, modelling it, but also demonstrating that in his death and resurrection something new is actually being accomplished by God that redefines

The Alexamenos Graffito

humanity. 'Father,' says Jesus as the nails are driven in, 'forgive them, for they do not know what they are doing.'

In common with Matthew and Mark, Luke tells us of the mocking directed towards Christ on the cross. Startlingly, just about the earliest depiction we have of the crucifixion is the so-called Alexamenos Graffito, which shows a figure with a donkey's head on a cross being worshipped by another, with the mocking inscription 'Alexamenos worships his God'.

We'll come back to that donkey: but Luke's Christ on the cross is far from a figure of fun, fully compos mentis and in command of the situation – an assumption reflected in the normal iconography of the crucifixion right up to the ninth century. In a scene unique to Luke, he not only forgives his tormentors but hears out the thieves crucified on either side of him.

The conversation allows Luke to introduce two vital points into the narrative. First, 'this man has done nothing wrong.' Crucifixion was regarded as a matter of disgrace by Romans and Jews alike. Luke is concerned at the very moment that it is being described to underline the innocence of Christ. Secondly, and more easily missed, is the saying about paradise. Almost in passing, as a matter of assumption, Jesus makes it clear that the cross for him is leading neither to oblivion nor hell. The story is not over; vindication is to follow; and in the face of such calm assurance the Satan has no power. 'At this moment', says Bishop Michael Marshall, 'Satan knows that he is defeated'.*

So Lord, who's the Donkey?
Is it you and those who bear your name?
Or those who find the whole Jesus thing
Just ridiculous?
Blessings, Lord, on Alexamenos.

WEEK 7

MAUNDY THURSDAY
What is our Witness?

Luke 23.44-47

It was now about the sixth hour, and darkness came over the whole land until the ninth hour, for the sun stopped shining. And the curtain of the temple was torn in two. Jesus called out with a loud voice, 'Father, into your hands I commit my spirit.' When he had said this, he breathed his last.

The centurion, seeing what had happened, praised God and said, 'Surely this was a righteous man.'

So we come to the moment of death. Nature mirrors spirit, and the sun withdraws it light. Creation as it were holds its breath, and then, even as the veil of the temple tears in two signalling the end of the old order and the end of its ritualised separation of God from his people, so at the same moment Jesus surrenders his human life boldly and voluntarily back to the Father. His words are not the cry of death but the Jewish prayer before sleep. 'Father, into your hands I commit my spirit.'

The watching centurion is made to witness not so much to Christ as son or a son of God, but to his righteousness. Luke is by no means abandoning Judaism for a Greek-style mystery religion, but seeing Judaism transformed into a way for all the world, and a way that could be commended to and by a Roman such as this soldier, whose retired compatriots populated the cities of Asia Minor.

We need to pause again for a moment and consider once more: who do we say it is that we are worshipping? And what are the implications of that for our world-view and our lives? Society around us is quick enough to make an ass of us, and indeed Christ, for our faith, and is at best ambivalent about the Christ-like life which refuses to pay back evil for evil.

It is always the Cross which brings the conversation between decent morality and Christian conviction to a crisis – its folly and waste to some, its implicit theological claims for others. But I dare not resort to a way of love that leaves out that Cross and crisis, and find that I have left out God.

So are we willing to stand in contradiction to the world around us, as Christ did on the cross? For a second time, consider your verdict, especially on this Maundy Thursday as we remember Jesus new commandment to love one another as he has loved us, so that the whole world might know that we are his disciples.

Eternal God,
the light of the minds that know you,
the joy of the wills that serve you;
grant us so to know you
that we may truly love,
and so to love you
that we may fully serve you,
whom to serve is perfect freedom,
in Jesus Christ our Lord.

After St Augustine

GOOD FRIDAY

Not the End – the Beginning

Luke 23.48-56

When all the people who had gathered to witness this sight saw what took place, they beat their breasts and went away. But all those who knew him, including the women who had followed him from Galilee, stood at a distance, watching these things.

Now there was a man named Joseph, a member of the Council, a good and upright man, who had not consented to their decision and action. He came from the Judean town of Arimathea and he was waiting for the kingdom of God. Going to Pilate, he asked for Jesus' body. Then he took it down, wrapped it in linen cloth and placed it in a tomb cut in the rock, one in which no one had yet been laid. It was Preparation Day, and the Sabbath was about to begin.

The women who had come with Jesus from Galilee followed Joseph and saw the tomb and how his body was laid in it. Then they went home and prepared spices and perfumes. But they rested on the Sabbath in obedience to the commandment.

The Cross is an event in history – but an event in our time too, and it demands a response both then and now. Luke pans the camera round, as it were, to show us some reactions.

The crowd at large is shown in conventional mourning, beating their breasts before leaving. We see it often enough. Those who know Jesus better stand to one side, watching and waiting, half-believing perhaps that this is not the end, without knowing quite what that means. I and probably you have spent not a little time watching and waiting, believing but not knowing.

Masaccio, *Crucifixion*

Joseph of Arimathea takes us back to the pious but 'quiet' Jews with whom Luke's gospel began. He uses his influence in a helpful way, without perhaps breaking cover as a follower of Christ. There are Josephs among us today.

And finally, the women. They have prepared their spices for the burial, but we are told explicitly that they follow the law and rest on the Sabbath. This sounds innocuous enough, but women were regarded as suspect witnesses and liable to uncleanness, so Luke is making a point. See too how Masaccio uses the new technique of perspective to force us to approach Christ in the company of the women, whether or not we feel comfortable with the emotion they are showing.

Jesus' mission was to inaugurate a new creation of the people of God in which the old barriers between Jew and Greek, male and female, slave and free would be broken down. We see it happening from the beginning. And we have to ask ourselves, is it still happening now? We do not come to church on Good Friday only to mark an event in the past, but to proclaim a reality for the present and offer a hope for the future – a hope of a better society, and a call to help give birth to it now.

In the Letter to the Ephesians we read that Christ has broken down the dividing wall of hostility and is our peace, and that in him we are joined together to make a holy Temple in which God's Spirit lives.* Consider now: what are the walls of division and hostility with which you live, behind which you stand – in your family life; in feuds where there should be friendships; in politics; in business; in plain prejudice; even in the life of the church. Consider them, and then set the sign of the cross over them to destroy them – and live the new life of reconciliation and peace.

Lord Jesus Christ,
you humbled yourself in taking the form of a servant,
and in obedience died on the cross for our salvation:
give us the mind to follow you
and to proclaim you as Lord and King,
to the glory of God the Father.

COMMON WORSHIP, Post-Communion Prayer for Holy Week *

EASTER EVE (Saturday)
Preparation Day

Luke 23.54-56

It was Preparation Day, and the Sabbath was about to begin. The women who had come with Jesus from Galilee followed Joseph and saw the tomb and how his body was laid in it. Then they went home and prepared spices and perfumes. But they rested on the Sabbath in obedience to the commandment.

Ivory Panel *The Empty Sepulchre* from Rome

The earliest representations of the Resurrection, such as the one on the little ivory plaque from fourth century Rome, now in the British Museum, do not show Christ. The whole point of the story, after all, is that he is not there. Instead, the door to the empty tomb stands tantalisingly ajar. Luke will go on to show how the women and men of the early church met Christ not head on, as it were, in ceremonies and rituals, but unexpectedly on the road, on the lakeside, in the garden, in their living room. He went before them into Galilee and he is going before us now into the Galilees of our own daily lives – and he will meet us there, alive and risen from the dead.

Easter Eve is a time of waiting and emptiness – but only because we are holding our breath with heaven for the great Alleluia that is about to come.

It is also a reminder though that every day is a Resurrection Day whether or not it is full of alleluias and the obvious presence of the Lord. We will shortly celebrate the Day of Easter, and the resurrection of Christ – but Christ's work of resurrection in the sense of bringing life to the dead, hope to the lost, wholeness to the broken, is for every day, as the same power that raised him is at work also in us.*

'He is here!' 'His Spirit is with us', as our Anglican liturgy has it, whether bidden or unbidden, sensed or not.

As we come to the end of this Lenten journey together, my greatest joy is that the bigger journey is only just beginning.

Try and take time then today to look back over Lent; to take stock of how you find yourself now; and prepare for the celebrations tomorrow, but for a lifetime of life in Christ as well.

 Almighty God, whose Son Jesus Christ is the resurrection and the life: raise us, who trust in him, from the death of sin to the life of righteousness, that we may seek those things which are above, where he reigns with you in the unity of the Holy Spirit, one God, now and for ever.

COMMON WORSHIP, Collect for the Fourth Sunday of Easter *

This is the last study session. It would be good to do something creative. I suggest making an Easter Garden. Depending on circumstances you could do this on your own, with a friend, as a group, or with family members or young neighbours. As you work on the garden, share your memories of Easter, and what you are planning to do this year – especially in your homes. For instance, my own memories go back to a daffodil-filled church (I can smell it now) on the Sheffield 'Flower Estate' where sadly there was barely a flower to be seen beyond the names of the roads. And each year now we build an Easter Tree in our hallway and decorate the dining table for a special meal.

Read Luke 23.54-56 again, the Preparation Day (it is Saturday's reading). What do you think the women are expecting to find when they come back to the tomb, and what do you think they will be doing? What are you expecting this Easter (and not just the eggs …: I mean

in your journey of faith)? What is dark in your life that you want to see made light? What speaks of death that needs that daffodil smell of life?

Gather by the garden to pray. The stone will probably be closed against the tomb's opening. Sometimes a candle is lit outside it to symbolise that this is not the end, but about to be a beginning. Pray for the stones that you want to see rolled back in your life, the life of others, and in the world.

EASTER DAY
TO ALL NATIONS

Alleluia!

Luke 24.1-8

On the first day of the week, very early in the morning, the women took the spices they had prepared and went to the tomb. They found the stone rolled away from the tomb, but when they entered, they did not find the body of the Lord Jesus. While they were wondering about this, suddenly two men in clothes that gleamed like lightning stood beside them. In their fright the women bowed down with their faces to the ground, but the men said to them, 'Why do you look for the living among the dead? He is not here; he has risen! Remember how he told you, while he was still with you in Galilee: 'The Son of Man must be delivered into the hands of sinful men, be crucified and on the third day be raised again.'' Then they remembered his words.

Black and white does not do justice the explosion which is Matthias Grünewald's *Resurrection* from the Isenheim Altarpiece (below). The real and surreal collide as he seeks to express the joy and power of the new life in Christ. The Resurrection is both an event in history and in eternity. The painter enters his own painting and makes it new. This is a day for celebration, for joy, for Life. Go for it!

Lord of all life and power,
who through the mighty resurrection of your Son
overcame the old order of sin and death
to make all things new in him:
grant that we, being dead to sin
and alive to you in Jesus Christ,
may reign with him in glory;
to whom with you and the Holy Spirit
be praise and honour, glory and might,
now and in all eternity.

COMMON WORSHIP, Collect for Easter Day *

EASTER MONDAY
Only Believe

Luke 24.9-12

When they came back from the tomb, they told all these things to the Eleven and to all the others. It was Mary Magdalene, Joanna, Mary the mother of James, and the others with them who told this to the apostles. But they did not believe the women, because their words seemed to them like nonsense. Peter, however, got up and ran to the tomb. Bending over, he saw the strips of linen lying by themselves, and he went away, wondering to himself what had happened.

A Lent book that does not stop at Easter! It is a gentle reminder that neither does our Easter faith … These extra studies during Easter Week give us the opportunity to carry our faith forward into the daily routine of year-round life.

The women take the news of the Resurrection back to the menfolk, who were perhaps already in hiding 'for fear of the Jews'. The men give them a hard time. They call the news 'nonsense' or 'an idle tale' – which takes us right back to the beginning of our study. What sort of story is this?

A family turned up in a church after seeing the Mel Gibson film of the Passion. They weren't sure about the answers, but they were sure that they had encountered the question.* A feature of our present post-modern culture is that we have become accustomed to taking in a huge variety of experiences and ideas, and not going on to resolve the question of their truth. This story, though, demands an answer – is Jesus raised from the dead? Is it history or not? We may not always feel comfortable either with the sharpness of the question, or with our own ability to answer it – but it is hard to avoid its necessity.

The first step in the journey beyond Easter for disciples then and now is to feel this imperative, to sense that this is not another passing insight but a permanent change in how we see things. European Football Fever recently gripped the city centre around me, with English flags everywhere. The flag of course carries a cross. We were all looking at it – though with enormously varied interpretations. Also on sale were some bizarre sunglasses with the lenses coloured with the same design. I had to try some on, and I wondered – what is it like to not just look at the cross, but look at life through it. The early literature I used to study and teach looked at life like that: I had to help post-modern students re-capture the way in which everything for the writers of those times took the core of our faith for granted, whether they were writing philosophy or history, theology or comic tales.

So, as the resurrection confronts us, are we going to look at it, and then get on with life, or know in our hearts that the whole of our life has now to be lived in its light?

Grünewald, *Resurrection*

I went to the opticians recently –
A regular checkup to make sure that dad's glaucoma
Isn't catching up with me too.
No problem!
OK – except for a bit of help with the small print ...
And then I saw those very strange specs:
I could hardly see through them.
And I wondered:
Even after all these years, Lord,
It takes an effort to look at things
In the light of the Cross,
In the light of your life.

EASTER TUESDAY
The Lord has Risen

Luke 24.13-35

Now that same day two of them were going to a village called Emmaus, about seven miles from Jerusalem. They were talking with each other about everything that had happened. As they talked and discussed these things with each other, Jesus himself came up and walked along with them; but they were kept from recognizing him.

He asked them, 'What are you discussing together as you walk along?'

They stood still, their faces downcast. One of them, named Cleopas, asked him, 'Are you only a visitor to Jerusalem and do not know the things that have happened there in these days?'

'What things?' he asked.

Caravaggio,
Supper at
Emmaus

'About Jesus of Nazareth,' they replied. 'He was a prophet, powerful in word and deed before God and all the people. The chief priests and our rulers handed him over to be sentenced to death, and they crucified him; but we had hoped that he was the one who was going to redeem Israel. And what is more, it is the third day since all this took place. In addition, some of our women amazed us. They went to the tomb early this morning but didn't find his body. They came and told us that they had seen a vision of angels, who said he was alive. Then some of our companions went to the tomb and found it just as the women had said, but him they did not see.'

He said to them, 'How foolish you are, and how slow of heart to believe all that the prophets have spoken! Did not the Christ have to suffer these things and then enter his glory?' And beginning with Moses and all the

Prophets, he explained to them what was said in all the Scriptures concerning himself.

As they approached the village to which they were going, Jesus acted as if he were going farther. But they urged him strongly, 'Stay with us, for it is nearly evening; the day is almost over.' So he went in to stay with them.

When he was at the table with them, he took bread, gave thanks, broke it and began to give it to them. Then their eyes were opened and they recognized him, and he disappeared from their sight. They asked each other, 'Were not our hearts burning within us while he talked with us on the road and opened the Scriptures to us?'

They got up and returned at once to Jerusalem. There they found the Eleven and those with them, assembled together and saying, 'It is true! The Lord has risen and has appeared to Simon.' Then the two told what had happened on the way, and how Jesus was recognized by them when he broke the bread.

The Emmaus disciples were accompanied on their journey, by each other and by Christ. As we work out our faith there is strength for us in doing the same, and not going it alone. Lent groups by definition end with Lent. But why not keep going? Together you can open the Scriptures, listen for the voice of Jesus, break the bread, sense his presence, and take the good news to others.

Which of us does not wish to find our hearts burning within us? To see the story behind the stories – of the Bible and of our own experiences? Feel how Caravaggio draws you into the wonder of the Emmaus meal by the dramatic gestures of the disciples and the contrasty lighting. This is life with a capital L, life in all its fullness – resurrection life.

If you are sensing that faith rise up in your heart now, step out, start walking: you'll not be walking alone.

Lord, show your people the road to blessedness, strengthened by the words of Christ, and united with the praises of his saints, so that in him we may come to see you face to face, O Lord and King of all.

Franciscan Office *

EASTER WEDNESDAY
The Peace of His Presence

Luke 24.36-43

While they were still talking about this, Jesus himself stood among them and said to them, 'Peace be with you.'

They were startled and frightened, thinking they saw a ghost. He said to them, 'Why are you troubled, and why do doubts rise in your minds? Look at my hands and my feet. It is I myself! Touch me and see; a ghost does not have flesh and bones, as you see I have.'

After Caravaggio, *The Incredulity of St Thomas* (detail)

When he had said this, he showed them his hands and feet. And while they still did not believe it because of joy and amazement, he asked them, 'Do you have anything here to eat?' They gave him a piece of broiled fish, and he took it and ate it in their presence.

I've tried to temper my enthusiasm for the journey of faith with the reminder that a commitment to discipleship is by no means an escape from struggle and questions. It is better seen as a commitment to one particular struggle, one particular question or set of questions, above all others. Of course the scriptures and creeds give us firm foundations – and we will come back to those tomorrow – but faith involves trust quite as much as knowledge, and trust is something that is never easy, and is increasingly difficult in fact in our present society.

These post-Resurrection stories in Luke's Gospel chronicle the struggle to faith of the first disciples. They found it hard to believe because they did not understand that here was the possibility, even the promise, of an event which was quite out of the ordinary.

They found it hard to believe because they were afraid and disheartened; because they mistrusted the witnesses; because they needed to see for themselves. And when they did see for themselves, they still found it hard to believe –a remarkable phrase in today's passage – because of their joy and amazement. They could not even trust their own senses.

We have to take this struggle seriously. The journey of faith is just that for nearly all of us – a whole series of small steps and encounters. Even if there are great turning points and overwhelming moments – and I can point to them in my own life – these are still embedded in a journey which is far from over. It isn't surprising that Thomas has been a most attractive role model in recent years, as his doubt is seen as affirmation rather than failure. He is not named in Luke's version of the story, but we can sense him in the background.

We do, though, have to read the whole story. The perplexities of the disciples are met by the very physical presence of Jesus. Look how Caravaggio emphasises the physicality of Thomas' touch, as his finger almost gruesomely explores the wound. His face is a picture (if you'll forgive the pun).

As we step out in faith our shared experience is that our sense of the presence of Christ is strengthened, and the gift of his peace is deepened. As, in an old phrase, we practise that presence, the bones of real daily living are clothed with the flesh of spiritual life. This is no ghost, no product of our imagination. It is exactly what Christ promised. 'I will be with you always, even to the end of time.'

Grant, Lord, that we may hold to you without parting,
worship you without wearying, serve you without failing;
faithfully seek you, happily find you, and forever possess you,
the only God, blessed, now and for ever.

St Anselm of Canterbury *

EASTER THURSDAY
The Scriptures Fulfilled

Luke 24.44-48

He said to them, 'This is what I told you while I was still with you: Everything must be fulfilled that is written about me in the Law of Moses, the Prophets and the Psalms.'

Then he opened their minds so they could understand the Scriptures. He told them, 'This is what is written: The Christ will suffer and rise from the dead on the third day, and repentance and forgiveness of sins will be preached in his name to all nations, beginning at Jerusalem. You are witnesses of these things.'

Three times! Amazingly Luke records the disciples as being taken through the Bible basics three times in this post-Resurrection period.

If Luke was, as I think he was, writing for the God-fearers dispersed through the Mediterranean world alongside the Jewish communities there, then a major plank in his evangelistic platform had to be to demonstrate that what had happened in the life, death and resurrection of Jesus was what was foretold in the Jewish scriptures.

It is surprising and reassuring by turns to see how the disciples both before and after the resurrection made such heavy weather of grasping the point! What that underlines is that grasping the point is not necessarily a straightforward thing to do. My own experience was that it took a fairly definitive encounter with the Holy Spirit before a lot of head knowledge of the Bible and already real faith travelled that short but critical distance to the heart and made a deeper sense.

I don't think this can be done 'by numbers'. The scriptures are given to us to be a wonderful foundation for our faith, but it is almost as if they have to discover us rather than we discover them, otherwise there is always a danger that we are pulling ourselves up by our own shoelaces rather than being lifted up by the Spirit.

Spencer, *The Resurrection, Cookham*

This means that somehow each of us has to encounter the Bible in our own way, stay in its company in a sort of courtship, wondering how the love affair will go. As we consider in this week's studies some of the hallmarks of the ongoing journey of faith – the basic step of belief, the accompanied journey, the presence of Christ (and tomorrow, the work of the Spirit) – we have to include the opening of the Scriptures and the opening of our minds to them.

Bible notes, Bible reading plans, listening to the Bible on CD, Bible study groups, following the Bible as it is read in church, reading the Bible in another language, scribbling your thoughts all over a Bible, studying the Bible's background – any or all of these might be right for you. As may be looking at the Bible in pictures. Take Stanley Spencer's *Resurrection* for instance. Would you really choose to include a Thames launch to take the resurrected to heaven? Why did he? What picture do you form in your mind as you read the scriptures?

Open my mind, Lord, to the pictures you want to show me.
And open the scriptures to renew my mind.

EASTER FRIDAY
Waiting for the Spirit

Luke 24.49-53

I am going to send you what my Father has promised; but stay in the city until you have been clothed with power from on high.'

When he had led them out to the vicinity of Bethany, he lifted up his hands and blessed them. While he was blessing them, he left them and was taken up

Giotto, *The Ascension of Christ*

into heaven. Then they worshiped him and returned to Jerusalem with great joy. And they stayed continually at the temple, praising God.

We've made it! This is the last daily study in the book – and as you guessed it's quite as much a beginning as an end.

The Ascension is not an easy subject to represent. The mediaeval versions which have the divine feet dangling from a cloud (carved versions were made too!) are rib-ticklingly amusing. Later ones can look like pious implausibilities. Giotto for me does a pretty good job – and what makes it work, I think, is his use of what feels like an eastern icon tradition in having Christ almost leap into the heavens, but with a much more western rootedness in the earthly life beneath. (Giotto's figures are never anything but solid.)

This gets right the dynamic nature of the relationship between earth and heaven, God and humanity. Christ ascends, and the Spirit will descend. Life is not lost but enlivened. The divine is not simply to be sought 'up there' but to be looked for, received and lived 'down here'.

So the disciples are explicitly commanded both to stay in the city and to look to be clothed with the power from on high, the Spirit at Pentecost, which will launch Luke's Acts.

I find this hugely encouraging. I was brought up in a serious Christian commitment to the city, to social concern and a lived-out faith. And I have experienced the work of God's Spirit in personal renewal as well. We are not meant to choose! There is something deeply out of kilter with the ecclesiastical politics which set one against the other. The Spirit is not given as a sort of private blessing. If we experience personal renewal in our faith, we are rightly called and even driven to help the church in its renewal (not disappear off into a separate sect). And as the church experiences renewal it is called and even driven to seek the renewing and transforming of the society around it – until that too is caught up into the kingdom of God and returns the glory to him in praise and thanksgiving.

We cannot and dare not try to live without the Spirit. We cannot and dare not keep it in the conventicle. Our pilgrim's journey begins and ends in the temple – but the way between lies through every nation, and on some very exciting roads. The Lord be with you as you follow the Way. His Spirit is with us!

Since, Lord, Thou dost defend
Us with Thy Spirit,
We know we at the end
Shall life inherit.
Then fancies flee away!
I'll fear not what men say;
I'll labour night and day
To be a pilgrim.

after John Bunyan *

References

viii On St Luke as a painter of the Virgin and Child, see also Neil MacGregor, *Seeing Salvation* (BBC, London 2000) pp. 86 and 88.

1 The storyteller was Kasi Khushnawaz, in Michael Wood's BBC TV series, *In the Footsteps of Alexander the Great* of 1997. See also Wood's book of the same name (BBC, London 1997) p.8.

1 The prayer is the refrain from Eucharistic Prayer D in *Common Worship: Services and Prayers for the Church of England* (Church House Publishing, London 2000) p.195.

5 See John Drury, *Painting the Word* (Yale University Press and the National Gallery, New Haven and London, 1999) pp.48-53.

5 Christopher Wordsworth's classic hymn *Gracious Spirit Holy Ghost*, of which this is the last verse, is in most standard hymnals, e.g. *Common Praise* 182, *New English Hymnal* 367. *Complete Mission Praise* 198 offers a different version of the hymn which does not include this verse.

7 John Rose's autobiography was privately published as *Traveller's Joy: The autobiography of John Rose* (J.S.Fordham, 1991).

7 Pat Uhl Howard's hymn *Canticle of the Gift (O what a Gift!)* is © The American Catholic Press and was originally published in *The Johannine Hymnal*. It can be found in *Complete Mission Praise* 526.

9 The original text of the play can be found in *The Wakefield Pageants* in the Towneley Cycle ed. A. C. Cawley (Manchester University Press, Manchester 1958) pp.43ff.

11 The Collect is from *Common Worship*, p.393.

13 This is part of the famous prayer of Richard of Chichester (1197-253) which begins 'Thanks be to thee.' The full text is on page 71.

15 The theology of the kingdom presented here draws on the important work of N.T. Wright in his multi-volume work *Christian Origins and the Question of God*, especially vol. 2, *Jesus and the Victory of God* (SPCK, London 1996).

17 I use two prayers attributed to Reinhold Niebuhr (1892-1971). He was an American theologian who taught at Union Theological Seminary and expounded a 'vital prophetic Christianity'. See *The Oxford Dictionary of the Christian Church*, 3rd edition ed. E. A. Livingstone (OUP, Oxford 1997) p.1153.

23 For the life of St Teresa of Avila (1515-82) see *ODCC* p.1589.

24 The resource pack *The Christ we Share* ed. Anne McConnell of USPG, 3rd ed. 2004 is published jointly by CMS, USPG and the Methodist Church. The pack includes 32 A5 colour images, activity sheets, a CD etc.

25 The Chaucer reference is obviously to his *Canterbury Tales*, available in many editions.

25 The Collect is from *Common Worship*, p.394.

27 The idea of the 'Pain-Bearer' sign is not mine, but I can no longer remember where I first encountered it. My thanks to the donor!

29 The reference is to Eric Berne's popular book, *Games People Play: The Psychology of Human Relationships* (first pub. 1964; my ed. Penguin, London 1968).

31 The prayer is from *Common Worship*, p.181.

33 The prayer is from *Common Worship*, p.182.

35 This prayer was attributed to St Francis on the card where I saw it, but it exists in several versions and the attribution is probably apocryphal.

37 The Collect is from the Church of England's *Book of Common Prayer* of 1662.

39 The Collect is from *Common Worship*, p.394.

42 I found the reference in *Rolling in the Aisles* by Murray Watts (MARC 1987) p.27.

43 The Collect is from the Communion Service in the Church of England's *Book of Common Prayer* of 1662.

45 Dag Hammarskjöld (1905-61) was a Swedish statesman and secretary-general of the UN. The prayer comes from his *Markings* written in 1957.

49 The reference is to T.S. Eliot's *Four Quartets*, Burnt Norton I.44 in *The Complete Poems and Plays of T.S. Eliot* (Faber and Faber, London 1969) p.172.

51 The prayer is attributed to Thomas More (1478-1535), possibly written in the Tower of London in the months before his execution. For More's biography see *ODCC* p.1114.

53 The Collect is from *Common Worship*, p. 396.

55 The prayer is a modernised version of one written by King Alfred for the end of his translation into Anglo-Saxon of Boethius' *On the Consolation of Philosophy*.

63 The Collect is from Evening Prayer in the Church of England's *Book of Common Prayer* of 1662.

67 The Collect is from *Common Worship*, p.396.

71 See under 13 above for Richard of Chichester's prayer.

75 The Valediction is a blessing at the end of the Alternative Service of Confirmation in the Church of England's *Book of Common Prayer with the Additions and Deviations proposed in 1928*. It was quoted by Her Majesty the Queen in her Millennium Christmas Broadcast of 2000.

77 For Niebuhr see note to p.17.

81 The Collect is from *Common Worship*, p.397.

82 'A certain man from Cyrene, Simon, the father of Alexander and Rufus ...', Mark 15.21.

87 Michael Marshall's point was made in an address to an Oxford Diocesan Conference.

91 'For he himself is our peace, who has made the two one and has destroyed the barrier, the dividing wall of hostility, by abolishing in his flesh the law with its commandments and regulations,' Ephesians 2.14.

91 The prayer is the post-Communion Collect for Palm Sunday and Holy Week from *Common Worship*, p.397.

93 '... his incomparably great power for us who believe. That power is like the working of his mighty strength, which he exerted in Christ when he raised him from the dead.' Ephesians 1.19-20. 'And if the Spirit of him who raised Jesus from the dead is living in you, he who raised Christ from the dead will also give life to your mortal bodies through his Spirit, who lives in you.' Romans 8.11.

93 The Collect is from *Common Worship*, p.402.

95 The Collect is from *Common Worship*, p.400.

96 The story of the family is a true one which came to me via the New Wine network.

99 The prayer is from *Celebrating Common Prayer: A Version of the Daily Office SSF* (Mowbray, London 1992) p.323.

101 The prayer is translated from one by St Anselm of Canterbury (1033-1109). For his biography see *ODCC* p.73.

105 The verse used as a prayer is from Percy Dearmer's adaptation *He who would valiant be* of John Bunyan's original hymn *Who would true valour see*. The adapted version is in many hymnals, e.g. *Complete Mission Praise* 224, *New English Hymnal* 372. The original version is in *Common Praise* 621.

Further Reading

There is no shortage of books about St Luke's Gospel. In my own studies I have tended to rely on the work of I. Howard Marshall for solid background information and detailed exegesis – see his *Luke – Historian and Theologian* (Paternoster, Exeter1970) and *The Gospel of Luke: A Commentary on the Greek Text* (Paternoster, Exeter 1978) in the *New International Greek Testament Commentary* series. For application of the gospel, I still enjoy William Barclay's *The Gospel of Luke* (St Andrew Press, Edinburgh 1953 – and many other editions) in the *Daily Study Bible* series; and now Tom Wright's *Luke for Everyone* (SPCK, London 2001). Wright's heavyweight theological works are mentioned in the references. There are many other very readable intermediate-level commentaries. They are helpfully surveyed by Steve Walton in *Biblical Studies Bulletin 6* (Grove Books, 1997) – though he is no fan of Barclay! Since theological backgrounds, methodological approaches, levels of detail and attitudes to application vary so much in both writers and readers, the best advice must be to look at several books and pick what helps you the most.

Religious Art is another huge field. The National Gallery's exhibition *Seeing Salvation* in the year 2000 was an excellent curtain-raiser, and both the exhibition catalogue *The Image of Christ* by Gabriele Finaldi (National Gallery, London 2000) and the BBC's accompanying series *Seeing Salvation* (available on videotape) and its book of the same name by Neil MacGregor (BBC, London 2000) are very good. MacGregor has discussions of the ivory plaque of the Resurrection (p.122 and plate 39: see also *Image* cat. no. 43), the *Man of Sorrows* (p.126 and plate 40 – cat. no. 44), and Grünewald's *Isenheim Resurrection* (p.185 and plate 58). *The Image of Christ* catalogue also reproduces and discusses Bosch's *Crowning with Thorns* (no. 45) and Spencer's *Resurrection, Cookham* (no. 79).

John Drury's *Painting the Word: Christian Pictures and their Meanings* (Yale University Press and the National Gallery, New Haven and London 1999) is another seminal work that has influenced me greatly, and it is beautifully illustrated in a way with which this present small work cannot compete! Fra Lippo Lippi's *Annunciation* is discussed in detail on pp. 48-53, della Francesca's *Nativity* on pp. 78-83, and Caravaggio's *Supper at Emmaus* on pp. 121-129. I have learnt and drawn from all these works extensively.

For more general background, I have found the *Oxford History of Art* series helpful – such as Robin Cormack's *Byzantine Art* (OUP, Oxford 2000) and also the *Art and Ideas* series by Phaidon – such as John Lowden's *Early Christian and Byzantine Art* (Phaidon, London and New York, 1997) on the same period. Phaidon are also issuing an excellent series of books collecting 120 or so illustrations of the same theme in chronological sequence, under one-word titles such as *Annunciation* (designed by Julia Hasting, Phaidon, London 2000).

For a general survey of the crucial Renaissance period, Andrew Graham-Dixon's *Renaissance* (University of California Press, Berkeley and Los Angeles 1999), published once again to accompany a BBC series of the same name, is both excellent and accessible. Just published for the mediaeval period, on CD, is *Images of Salvation: The Story of the Bible through Mediaeval Art* edited by Dee Dyas, from the Christianity and Culture project based at St John's College, Nottingham (www.york.ac.uk/inst/cms/candc). I suggest you contact the project for distribution details.

An older general volume which still has some interest is Eric Newton and William Neil's *The Christian Faith in Art* (Hodder and Stoughton, London 1966), and *The Bible in Art* by Richard Mühlenberger (Portland House, New York 1990/1 2 vols and other edd.) is one of the better coffee-table size books. The Van Gogh *Good Samaritan* is discussed on p.89 of the New Testament volume. Jane Dillenberger, *Style and Content in Christian Art* (SCM Press, London 1965) is an example of a more discursive approach to the subject, and *The Oxford Companion to Christian Art and Architecture* by Peter and Linda Murray (OUP, Oxford 1998) and the *Dictionary of Christian Art* by Diane Apostolos-Cappadona (Lutterworth, Cambridge 1995) are useful reference books.

As with studies on Luke, there is far more out there to read than I have seen or can mention here, and a trawl in a good second-hand-bookshop can be rewarding!

List of Illustrations and Websites

In the following list the full names and dates of the artists and works are given together with their present location and appropriate copyright and permission details. The website of the gallery or museum is also given, where one is known to us, and where this does not include a colour reproduction of the work a further reference is also given which will lead to one. Copyright restrictions should be borne in mind in using all web reproductions.

PAGE

ix Marten de Vos (1532-1603), *St Luke Painting the Virgin Mary* 1602
(Koninklijke Museum voor Schome Kunsten, Antwerp)
© Koninklijke Museum voor Schome Kunsten, Antwerp
http://museum.antwerpen.be/kmska/
http://www.biblical-art.com/artwork.asp?id_artwork=6865&showmode=
Full#artwork

4 Fra Filippo Lippi (1406-1469), *The Annunciation* c.1450-3
[also used as detail on pages 5 & 10]
(National Gallery, London)
© National Gallery, London
http://www.nationalgallery.org.uk/cgi-bin/WebObjects.dll/Collection
Publisher.woa/wa/work?workNumber=ng666

6 Mariotto Albertinelli (1474-1515), *The Visitation* 1503
(Galleria degli Uffizi, Florence)
© Photo SCALA Florence 1996 – courtesy of the Ministero Beni e
Att. Culturali
http://www.uffizi.firenze.it
http://www.biblical-art.com/artwork.asp?id_artwork=3778&showmode=
Full#artwork

9 Piero della Francesca (1415/20-1492), *The Nativity* 1470-5 [detail]
(National Gallery, London)
© National Gallery, London
http://www.nationalgallery.org.uk/cgi-bin/WebObjects.dll/Collection
Publisher.woa /wa/work?workNumber=ng908

13 Jacopo Bassano (c.1510-1592), *The Miraculous Draught of Fishes* 1545
    [also used as detail on pages 11 & 17]
    (National Gallery of Art, Washington)
    © Board of Trustees, National Gallery of Art, Washington
    http://www.nga.gov/cgi-bin/pinfo?object=95581+0+none

14 Michelangelo Merisi da Caravaggio (1573-1610), *The Call of
    Matthew* 1599-1600
    (Contarelli Chapel, San Luigi dei Francesi, Rome)
    © Photo SCALA Florence 1990
    http://www.wga.hu/frames-e.html?/html/c/caravagg/04/
    http://www.biblical-art.com/artwork.asp?id_artwork=1297&showmode
    =Full#artwork

21 James Tissot (1836-1902), *The Confession of Peter* 1886-96
    [also used as detail on page 24]
    (Print from The Life our Saviour Jesus Christ, McClure Tissot, New
    York 1899) With thanks to Rolf Earling Staerk of Biblical Art for the
    photograph from his collection.
    http://www.biblical-art.com/artwork.asp?id_artwork=1425&showmode
    =Full#artwork

22 Raffaello Sanzio (1483-1520), *The Transfiguration* 1516-20
    (Pinacoteca Apostolica Vaticano, Rome)
    © Photo SCALA Florence 1990
    http://mv.vatican.va/3_EN/pages/x-Schede/PINs/PINs_Sala08_05_035.html

25 Rembrandt Harmenszoon van Rijn (1606-1669), *The Return of the
    Prodigal Son* c.1662
    [also used as detail on pages 32 and 38]
    (The Hermitage State Museum, St Petersburg)
    http://www.hermitagemuseum.org

26 Vincent Van Gogh (1853-90), *The Good Samaritan* 1890
    [also used as detail on page 38]
    (Rijksmuseum Kröller-Müller, Otterlo, Netherlands)
    © stichting kröller-müller museum
    http://www.kmm.nl
    http://www.biblical-art.com/artwork.asp?id_artwork=9710&showmode
    =Full#artwork

31 Vie de Jésus Mafa, *The Poor Invited to the Feast* (detail) 1973-7
[also used as detail on page 38]
(Print from Vie de Jésus Mafa)
All rights reserved: Vie de Jésus MAFA, 24 rue de Maréchal Joffre,
F-78000 Versailles. *Vie de Jésus Mafa* is a coherent set of pictures
illustrating 61 scenes of the New Testament. They are published as
posters and on videotape. They have been shared with the world
for more than 25 years with ongoing success, especially where
people have a special feeling for a black Jesus in an African
surrounding.
www.jesusmafa.com

34 German Woodcut, *The Shrewd Manager* 1516
(From Das Plenarium oder Ewangely buoch, 1516.)
The Pitts Theology Library, Candler School of Theology, Emory
University
www.pitts.emory.edu/ woodcuts/1516Cath/00001574.jpg

41 The Dome of the Rock, Jerusalem 1990
(Photo David Thomson)

44 James Ensor (1860-1949), *Christ's Entry in Brussels in 1889* 1888
Oil on canvas, 252.7 x 430.5cm
[also used on page 52]
(The J. Paul Getty Museum, Los Angeles)
© Estate of James Ensor/Artists' Rights Society (ARS) New York
http://www.getty.edu/art/collections/objects/o932.html

46 El Greco (1541-1614), *Christ Driving out Traders from the Temple*
1600 [detail]
(National Gallery, London)
© National Gallery, London
http://www.nationalgallery.org.uk/cgi-bin/WebObjects.dll/Collection
Publisher.woa/wa/work?workNumber=ng1457

48 Gustave Doré (1832-1883), *The Widow's Mite* 1865
(From the Doré edition of La Sainte Bible, 1865)
http://www.biblical-art.com/artwork.asp?id_artwork=2013&showmode
=Full#artwork

55 Emil Nolde (1867-1956), *The Last Supper* 1909
    [also used as detail on pages 59 & 66]
    (Statens Museum for Kunst, Copenhagen)
    © Photo DOWIC Fotografi
    www.smk.dk
    http://www.beloit.edu/~classics/main/courses/fyi2000/museum/20thcentury/

60 Gethsemane Chapel, Coventry Cathedral 1956-62
    Photo reproduced by kind permission of the Chapter of Coventry
    Cathedral
    For another image see:
    http://www.coventrycathedral.org/education/edu_image_1.htm

63 Giotto di Bondone (1266-1336), *The Kiss of Judas* 1304-6
    [also used as cover illustration]
    (Cappella degli Scrovegni, Padua)
    © Photo SCALA Florence 1990
    http://www.cappelladegliscrovegni.it/index_eng.asp
    http://www.biblical-art.com/artwork.asp?id_artwork=2167&Showmode
    =Full#artwork

69 Umbrian Master, *The Man of Sorrows* c.1260
    [also used as detail on page 70]
    (National Gallery, London)
    © National Gallery, London
    http://www.nationalgallery.org.uk/cgi-bin/WebObjects.dll/Collection
    Publisher.woa/wa/work?workNumber=ng6573

72 Hieronymus Bosch (fl.1474-1516), *Christ Mocked* c.1490-1500
    [also used as detail on pages 75 & 80]
    (National Gallery, London)
    © National Gallery, London
    http://www.nationalgallery.org.uk/cgi-bin/WebObjects.dll/Collection
    Publisher.woa/wa/work?workNumber=ng4744

78 Sarcophagus of Domitilla. *Christ before Pilate* (detail) mid 4th cent.
    [also used as detail on page 77]
    (Museo Pio Cristiano, Vatican, Rome)
    © Photo SCALA Florence 1990
    http://www.christusrex.org/www1/vaticano/PC3-Sarc.jpg

82 Jacopo Bassano (c.1510-1592), *The Way to Calvary* 1545-50
(National Gallery, London)
© National Gallery, London
http://www.nationalgallery.org.uk/cgi-bin/WebObjects.dll/Collection
Publisher.woa/wa/work?workNumber=ng6490

84 Marc Chagall (1887-1985), *White Crucifixion* 1938
(Art Institute of Chicago)
© The Art Institute of Chicago/Artists' Rights Society (ARS) New York
http://www.artic.edu/aic/rights/search/.portweb?quickfind=E09176&te
plate=Preview&catalog=Sample

87 *The Alexamenos Graffito* dated to 1st-3rd cents
[also used as detail on page 88]
(Kircherian Museum at the Collegio Romano, Rome)
http://www.aug.edu/augusta/iconography/2003additions/alexamenos
Graffito.html

90 Masaccio [Tommaso di Ser Giovanni di Mone] (1401-28?),
Crucifixion
[also on title page]
(Museo Nazionale di Capodimonte, Naples)
© Photo SCALA Florence 2000 – courtesy of the Ministero Beni e
Att. Culturali
http://www.cib.na.cnr.it/remuna/capod/indice.html
http://www.biblical-
art.com/artwork.asp?id_artwork=5309&showmode=Full#artwork

92 Ivory Panel from Rome, *The Empty Tomb* 4th cent
[also used on page 94]
(British Museum)
© The Trustees of the British Museum
http://www.thebritishmuseum.ac.uk/compass

97 Matthias Grünewald (c.1480-1528), *The Resurrection*
(from *the Isenheim altarpiece*) 1512-16 [also used as detail on page 95]
(Musée d'Unterlinden, Colmar, France)
© Photo Bridgeman Art Library
http://www.musee-unterlinden.com/francais/collections/retable/index.html

98 Michelangelo Merisi da Caravaggio (1573-1610), *Supper at Emmaus* 1601
(National Gallery, London)
© National Gallery, London
http://www.nationalgallery.org.uk/cgi-bin/WebObjects.dll/Collection
Publisher.woa/wa/work?workNumber=ng172

100 Copy of Michelangelo Merisi da Caravaggio (1573-1610),
The Incredulity of St Thomas [detail]
(Galleria degli Uffizi, Florence)
© Photo SCALA Florence 1990 – courtesy of the Ministero Beni e
Att. Culturali
http://www.uffizi.firenze.it/ [no image]
The original of 1602-3 is in the Sanssouci, Potsdam
http://www.biblical-art.com/artwork.asp?id_artwork=2682&showmode
=Full#artwork

103 Stanley Spencer (1891-1959), *The Resurrection, Cookham* 1924-7
(Tate Gallery, London)
© Tate, London 2004
http://www.tate.org.uk/britain/exhibitions/spencer/room2.htm &
http://www.tate.org.uk/servlet/ViewWork?workid=13675&searchid=16481

104 Giotto di Bondone (1266-1336), *The Ascension of Christ* 1304-6
(Cappella degli Scrovegni, Padua)
© Photo SCALA Florence 1990
http://www.cappelladegliscrovegni.it/index_eng.asp
http://www.biblical-art.com/artwork.asp?id_artwork=2701&Showmode
=Full#artwork

A Journey with John

A Holy Week Bible Study

by David Thomson

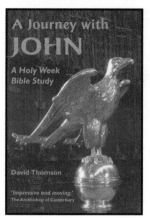

'David Thomson led the cathedral congregation in Carlisle, during Holy Week 2003, through St John's Gospel as it examines the wonder of the passion of Jesus. This book is based on that corporate journey. The printed word cannot capture the mystery of those evenings as together we followed the way of suffering, but it provides the tools whereby all may share something of the experience. I commend this small book to all who seek to deepen their understanding of the events of Holy Week – the Great Week – and to walk with Jesus the way of the cross.'

Graeme Knowles, *Bishop of Sodor and Man*

'These are very impressive and moving pieces. They capture something of the real drama and tension and depth of John's gospel and really drive the reader into the heart of the text. I found them very nourishing indeed.'

Rowan Williams, *Archbishop of Canterbury*

'This is a searching and beautiful Holy Week approach to the great and terrible gifts of Good Friday and Easter Sunday, and it leads us steadily into a deeper understanding of, and greater thankfulness for, the wonderful grace of God through his Son Jesus Christ.'

Ruth Etchells, *formerly Principal, St John's College with Cranmer Hall, University of Durham*

'David Thomson has a lovely gift of awakening our imagination with exciting images. As he takes us through the familiar narratives of St John, weaving his parallels with the story, he challenges our own response to the love and glory of the King. So stimulating is his writing that he made me want to read and ponder; and then to read and ponder again. For individuals or for groups these chapters will be a rewarding study.'

Graham Dow, *Bishop of Carlisle*

Authentic LIFESTYLE

£2.99   ISBN: 1-85078-561-9
210 x 148mm, 40pp, wire stitched,
www.authenticmedia.co.uk